Thornton Wilder and His Public

THORNTON WILDER
AND
HIS PUBLIC

Amos Niven Wilder

Fortress Press
Philadelphia

Published by Fortress Press
Philadelphia

First published 1980

Library of Congress Cataloging in Publication Data

Wilder, Amos Niven, 1895-
  Thornton Wilder and his public.

  Bibliography:
  1. Wilder, Thornton Niven, 1897-1975.
  2. Authors, American – 20th century – Biography.
  I. Title.
  PS3545.I345Z96   818'.5'209 [B] 79-26564
  ISBN 0-8006-0636-1

8291D80   Printed in the United States of America   1-636

To Isabel Wilder

CONTENTS

FOREWORD

SEVERAL KINDS OF PROMPTINGS have led me to initiate and develop this essay. One was that kind of interest in family history which often comes to the fore as we grow older. Uncovering early strata of family papers, letters, and photographs quickened the retrospect.

Since Thornton was only a year and a half younger than myself our associations were close in childhood and in early schooling. Though my two years at Oberlin College preceded his, we shared that same experience, including that of a great teacher of literature, Charles H. A. Wager. Though Thornton was not like myself overseas in World War I, we had had summer farming experience together and roomed together in our senior year at Yale (1910–1920) in Connecticut Hall. At Yale we shared such common literary excitements as the teaching of Jack Adams, Berdan, Phelps, and Tinker, the *Yale Literary Magazine,* and the Elizabethan Club where our friends included Steve Benét, John Farrar, and Wilmarth Lewis.

All through these earlier years, reflecting the literary interests of the family, including our sisters, our correspondence testified to new reading discoveries and writing projects. In the home, Walter Scott, Dickens, and Thackeray had been read aloud. As children we had taken part in the mob scenes of the classic drama enacted in the Greek Theater at Berkeley. In college we had heard Vachel Lindsay read

''The Congo,'' and seen the Abbey Theater do plays of Lady Gregory and Synge.

Though Thornton and I were not twins, I have always felt that there was some sort of occult affinity in my makeup for his fabulation, like the telepathic understanding between Manuel and Esteban in *The Bridge of San Luis Rey*. Incidentally I recall here in that connection that a Viennese psychiatrist and authority on the special mentality of twins wrote to him asking where he had learned so much about this phenomenon. Thornton could only reply that in our time at Oberlin College there were identical twin brothers among our fellow students whom he had observed.

As himself a twin who lost a brother at birth, he was predisposed to fascination with this relationship. Indeed one could hazard that he was haunted all his life by this missing alter ego. Thus he plays with the afterlife of this twin in the dual *persona* suggested by the title of his last novel, *Theophilus North*, ''North,'' of course, representing an anagram for Thornton. In this way he was able to tease both himself and the reader as to the borderlands between autobiography and fable.

In Thornton's writing there are furthermore motifs which I recognize on the basis of shared experience. In Act II of *The Skin of Our Teeth* the stage directions call for a weather signal whose successive black disks hung on a mast will move finally from warning of a hurricane to that of the Deluge or end of the world. When we were children in Hong Kong we were much impressed with a similar warning system, before the days of sirens, erected at the port. As I recall, large balls were exposed on a yardarm especially as a warning of bad weather to the hundreds of Chinese junks in the harbor. The climax was reached with four balls indicating a typhoon, and we experienced that at least once.

Though our European study years after college diverged, we later were associated, though at different times, with the exchange set up by Robert Hutchins between the University of Chicago and the University of Frankfurt. I shall return to this below. Though, also, in this period our callings diverged, yet even as concerns theology he could sometimes be ahead of me, as for example in appreciation of the Roman liturgy. He it was, moreover, who introduced me to Kierkegaard. In that process of extrication from what Hutchins called "the late foam-rubber period of American Protestantism" which our generation had to work through, Thornton was always alerting me to domains, sensitivities, and austerities which were missing in that tradition of piety.

Another factor prompting me to write this essay relates to my long interest as a theologian in modern letters. This concern arose first of all as a need to come to terms after World War I with the shocks and disenchantments of the period and with the revolution of language demanded by the situation, not least in religion. In my later several volumes devoted to modern writers I had never included his plays and novels.

I knew that very early in the Foreword to *The Angel That Troubled the Waters* (1928) he had written:

> I hope, through many mistakes, to discover the spirit that is not unequal to the elevation of the great religious themes, yet which does not fall into a repellent didacticism.

I recognized that in his novel *The Woman of Andros* (1930), in the opening and closing paragraphs, he presents the fable as a study of love in the ancient world anticipating the advent of Christianity. So *The Alcestiad,* first played in Edinburgh as *A Life in the Sun* in 1955, presents a heroine of antiquity, a "servant of servants," through whose vicarious death and return to life and eventual apotheosis the gates of Hades are shaken as a pledge for the future.

I always felt that my brother's major works represented an artistic and therefore oblique, though critical, affirmation of the great traditions of the West, classical and biblical. Much criticism has not known what to make of such affirmation in our period, or of the diverse strategies and forms in which it was evoked. Even if these were seen as masterly in invention and sophistication they fell outside what was considered to be the main line of modernist achievement and its proper iconoclasm.

I have therefore found it timely to consider these aspects of Thornton's work and his place in modern letters. As one who has so long defended the modern classics and their succession right down to Samuel Beckett, especially as one writing for traditional readers, I find it specially intriguing to explain the seeming hiatus between that whole movement and my brother's writing and public.

But this leads to fundamental and prior questions as to the modern world and its quests. Perhaps the iconoclasms of modern thought and modern art, granted their merits and masterpieces, have forfeited too much of the ancient heritage—with which they have indeed wrestled —and too much of that deeper continuity with an elder world and an abiding humanity which can still nourish us. Perhaps, as contemporary observers as various as Lionel Trilling, Octavio Paz, and George Steiner suggest, the whole great movement gives signs of diminishing returns or has even reached its term. In this light the traditionalism of Thornton Wilder—all the more because he was fully versed in modern sophistications—may be seen as calling attention to precious aspects of our humanity not on the main agenda of his contemporaries.

In this connection one further consideration has prompted my essay. It has to do with the special situation of the American writer. The focus of our intellectuals and critics and many of our artists has understandably been determined by worldwide and cosmopolitan cultural factors. Modernism in the arts and in sensibility has had its great antecedents abroad. It has of course related itself to our New-World situation. But the moral and imaginative climate here is stubbornly different. The pervasive archetypes and mythology of our society have a contribution to make to our modern quests. This is why I make so much in what follows of the grass-roots and religious influences in my brother's background and outlook. This is one dimension of his work which is uncongenial to avant-garde circles, but which may well relate him to deeper sources which are universal.

Critical discussion of Thornton's work in this country, to make another point, shows very little acquaintance with the response to it abroad, especially in Germany. Indeed, his immense vogue there was misconstrued on this side. What has been interesting about his appeal to German readers and theater audiences was not only the resonance of his native American archetypes but the level and extent of the critical discussion given to his drama and fiction. If social and political factors after World War II partly explain this, notably in the case of the extraordinary impact of *The Skin of Our Teeth,* one has to look further for a full explanation. Intellectual and artistic life in Germany, the terms of moral and cultural debate, were not so dominated by modernist ideology as in Paris and elsewhere. The old-world humanism in those strata which had suffered through the Nazi years was richer and less eroded.

I had occasion to take in this situation when I taught two semesters at the University of Frankfurt in 1951 and 1952 and visited both the theological faculties and the English seminars in other German universities. On my first arrival at Frankfurt Thornton wrote me and hailed my initiation into −

> that state of mind which is Germany. It's a wonderful and irreplaceable experience, not that there's anything *réjouissant* about it but *weltgeschichtliche Stimmung* [world-historical exhilaration] ... it expands the mind with awe, that's all I venture to say − and not primarily with pity nor admiration ... part of my joy in your going there is that now you must share my inarticulateness about IT − about Europe in dismay, irresolution, and horror − together with the elements of hope and continuity. To not be able to tell it is like a burden of guilt.

What Thornton here speaks of as *weltgeschichtliche Stimmung* points to the climate which could specially appreciate his writing and his personal contacts. This included the living sense of the classics and antiquity but also those dimensions of good and evil, freedom and fate, which had so recently convulsed Central Europe. In short, both the scholars and the audiences of Germany were well situated to appraise, on the one hand, the new dramaturgy and, on the other, the old moralities of Thornton's plays.

Here in this country, while there has always been a wide public with a similar discernment and response, the situation in criticism has been more complex. Both in aesthetics and in social as well as political thought the task of renewal has had first claim, given the massive traditional conformities and Philistinisms which persist. But some circles have made of iconoclasm a program and way of life.

Where modernism had been an exploration and a debate grounded in the tradition it could later all too easily become a dogma. Where the best of our students of culture and our artists have maintained their openness to a complex reality and heritage, in other circles narrower and narrower axioms prevail. Especially in a time which many identify as "postmodern" and "apocalyptic," simplifications should be shunned. What shall one then say of a critic who can sum up the cultural situation in America by writing that "an imposing Puritanism has been sublimed into IBM machinery"?* Here speaks the consistent ideologue, writing about modernist and postmodern fiction. But surely even today America has other visages than this, and Puritanism other and more fertile sequels.

In writing what follows I have also been aware, finally, of recent attention to my brother's work and career, especially following his death in December 1975. In this connection I quote from the moving tribute paid to him by Emil Staiger at the 1976 proceedings in Bonn of the Order, Pour le Mérite, of which he was a member. I also cite with appreciation the very perceptive address interpreting Thornton's place in modern letters made by Franz H. Link in the memorial observance arranged at Freiburg by the English-American Seminar of the University in association with local theater groups. Link has also dealt with Wilder's drama in his *Dramaturgie der Zeit* (1977). Aspects of his fiction are treated in Link's *Stilanalysen amerikanischer Erzählkunst* (1970).

In this country, besides the Memorial Service at Yale in which several of my brother's friends took part, there have been a number of interesting developments. In my essay I speak of the recent publication of his play, *The Alcestiad,* now for the first time available in English. Portions of the opera based on this play, composed by Louise Talma, with Thornton's libretto, and produced in Frankfurt in 1962, were sung at the Yale Music School in March 1976. Most recent has been the inauguration of an annual Thornton Wilder Memorial Lecture at the German School in Washington, D.C. In conversation with the students of the school, the first lecturer, Henry Kissinger,

---

*Marcus Klein, *After Alienation: American Novels in Mid-Century.* Cleveland, 1965, p. 295.

spoke of the impression made on him when, as a young man, he saw *The Skin of Our Teeth* in 1946 in Darmstadt in a bombed theater in a bombed city. That challenge to human survival he would never forget.

Also very recent (March 1978) has been the television production of four of the "Three Minute Plays for Three Persons" from *The Angel That Troubled the Waters* (1928) by the University of Wisconsin Theater Department Faculty. Under the caption, "Producing the Unproducible," even such a playlet as "And the Sea Shall Give Up Its Dead" was impressively rendered with the professional help of WHA-TV and the Milwaukee Repertory Theater. This venture will have wide distribution through public television.

The most recent book-length study of my brother has been Richard Goldstone's *Thornton Wilder: An Intimate Portrait* which came out shortly before his death. The author's *Paris Review* interview, "Thornton Wilder: The Art of Fiction," published in 1957, had been admirable. Some of the things Thornton says in it, however, seem to me to undercut aspects of the *Portrait*, especially as regards his family background. The book is in many respects highly informative. The author has marshaled a large documentation about his subject's career, his writings, and their reception. As one who had direct contact with my brother during his service in the Air Intelligence in World War II Goldstone illuminates this phase. Their contacts continued for a considerable period. For some reason this relation was later broken off.

As the author says in his Foreword, what began as a critical study with biographical background turned into a detailed portrait. But the biography appears, at least to a member of the family, to be skewed, apart from a good number of factual errors, and the portrait to be partial. So far as Thornton's private papers and letters were concerned the author had access only to those outside the family. One misses in the book adequate treatment of my brother's contacts and activities in Germany and the impact there of his addresses and writings.

My own chief issue with the book, however, arises in connection with the author's view of the "Puritan" influence on my brother and its handicaps. This is related to the unbalanced picture afforded of our

THORNTON WILDER AND HIS PUBLIC/

father. This leads to extravagant ventures into psychobiography.
Surely one has to use a fine microscope on Wilder's writings to find
parricide spinning the plot! Such a main study of my brother should
be in the hands of someone more congenial to his humanism and to
his own kind of Americanism. In reading the book one sometimes
wonders whether Goldstone really enjoys Thornton's work. I am
reminded of how unwise it was for Edgar Lee Masters to undertake a
biography of Vachel Lindsay.

Nevertheless I suppose that we should be glad that someone has
done the spade work represented in the documentation here of many
particulars, going beyond those shorter manuals heretofore available.
It is to be hoped, however, that students in high school and college
and other readers will not get their main impression of Thornton and
his work from this available source alone. To this end the present, no
doubt partial, essay by a brother may make some contribution.

A number of critics like Malcolm Cowley have remarked upon the
lack of thoroughgoing and substantive studies in this country of my
brother's novels and plays. This situation, again, raises a number of
interesting questions about the focus and scale of much contemporary
criticism. There appear to be moral ingredients and universal motifs
in Wilder's work which elude their tools and canons. Preoccupation
not simply with the *Zeitgeist* but with the dominant movement of
emancipation in our epoch leaves out of account works that reflect
deeper continuities. My brother's appeal to the unmodern, either that
of the past and the timeless, or that of the anonymous multitudes, can
only appear reactionary or untimely. The fact is they do not know
what to do with him.

But of course these issues should be and can be spelled out in terms
of a more adequate and sophisticated attention to Wilder's fabulation
and dramaturgy. And it is just this which is so far lacking.* But the
parameters of such criticism must be more profoundly humanistic
and catholic than those which characterize much of our current

---

*I would, however, call attention to the fact that one of the continuing seminars of the Mod-
ern Language Association (Seminar 4: Literature and Religion) gave its attention at the
1970 meeting to Thornton's novel, *The Eighth Day* (1967). Five illuminating essays on the
book, edited by Paul Schluter, were published in mimeographed form by the University of

practice, shaped as it is by particular aesthetic and cultural legacies. It is quite possible for a critic with these commitments to characterize *The Cabala* and *Heaven's My Destination* as Wilder's "only indisputably good works," while at the same time observing that "his streak of vulgarity and pseudoprofundity early emerged in *The Bridge of San Luis Rey,* a pretentious pseudomodern novel that reached its big readership target with distressingly unerring ease." He adds: "His many plays (the most famous are *Our Town* and *The Skin of Our Teeth*) are good theater but they are empty of real thought."* My point here is that much going criticism can appreciate the virtuosity and aestheticism of *The Cabala* just as it can lack a sense of the *humanum* and the dramaturgy of "world theater" in the two plays. The recurrent invidious slurs at Wilder's popularity betray a defensive elitism whose more serious limitation lies in its disesteem for the greater public, those multitudes who speak through *Our Town.*

As an example of the kind of critical exploration which could well be pursued by Americans I call attention to the most recent example of such study of my brother's work in Germany. It is a lengthy canvass by Horst Oppel of the impact and reception of his writing in German-speaking Europe, "Thornton Wilder in Deutschland: Wirkung und Wertung seines Werkes im deutschen Sprachraum."** The author is interested in such questions as Wilder's early contacts with German expressionist theater, and the similarities of his dramaturgy with that of Brecht as well as its divergence. He scrutinizes early contacts of the American writer with such figures as Max Reinhardt, Max Frisch, Ernst Junger, Hans Egon Holthusen, Gottfried Benn, and Dürrenmatt, or their responses, favorable and unfavorable, to his work.

Evansville. Evansville, Indiana. At the 1976 meeting of the MLA a special session with the topic, "Thornton Wilder: 1897–1975," was organized by Dalma H. Brunauer of Clarkson College of Technology, who edited five perceptive papers on his writing in similar form. Attention should also be called to a paper by Douglas Charles Wixson, Jr., "The Dramatic Techniques of Thornton Wilder and Bertolt Brecht: A Study in Comparison," published in *Modern Drama* XV, no. 2 (September 1972).

*M. Semour-Smith, *Who's Who in Twentieth Century Literature*. New York, 1976, p. 394.

***Abhandlungen der Klasse der Literatur/Akademie der Wissenschaften und der Literatur; Jg. 1976/77, no. 3. Mainz., 1977, pp. 1-31.*

This kind of approach is concerned not only with whether Wilder's work is optimistic or pessimistic, moralistic or didactic, but with technical and formal aspects of his art, questions of genre and method. The author notes a recurrent *topos* in the writings, that of descent to the underworld or converse with the dead, and reminds us of its contemporary use by such writers as Cocteau, Sartre, Elmore Rice, and Dylan Thomas. Another literary strategy worthy of comparative study to which he calls attention is the combination of catastrophe and farce, as in *The Skin of Our Teeth,* and even in *Heaven's My Destination,* which, I would add, is a compositional structure more serious than irony, and one that rises above the didactic.

Oppel's study calls attention to another factor in my brother's extraordinary impact in Germany, especially after World War II. Here it is a question of those intangible preconditions in a society and in a wide public which can account for this kind of resonance. No doubt the phenomenon was altogether exceptional with the production of *The Skin of Our Teeth* in postwar Germany.

> Sometimes, though but rarely in the annals of literature, a historical crisis, a deeply involved public and a drastic dramatization of the situation come into total conjunction. Such was the timeliness of Thornton Wilder's most powerful play.*

> With reference to the relation of the theater audience or reader to the literary work one can only speak here of an "identification-experience," such as can only rarely be registered of such extent and intensity.**

But the phenomenal appeal of Wilder's work over a considerable period was not confined to this one play. In any case Oppel is led to the kind of questions which could also interest American criticism with reference to the author of *Our Town.* These relate to the sociology of literary taste and to those hidden factors of *Rezeptionsästhetik,* or audience sensibility, for whose operation my brother's impact in Germany offers "a classical case."

**P. 12. citing L. M. Price, *The Reception of United States Literature in Germany.* *Chapel Hill, 1966, P. 174.*

This domain, of course, immediately confronts us with the problem of nonliterary factors in an author's appeal. I cite further on in this essay the claim by an American critic that the infatuation with Thornton Wilder's work and image in Germany in the late forties and fifties traced to quasi-political causes and to instability in the German psyche. Oppel rejects this diagnosis. Wilder's success rested rather upon those dynamics of literary response (formulated by L. L. Shücking) according to which the widest reception is accorded to works "which exhibit what is already known in new form and which actualize whatever is cherished and trusted." In the Central European situation Oppel identifies this living resource evoked by Wilder as the traditions of antiquity, Christian ethos, and the European cultural legacy.

But these, evidently, are only general pointers to an available past, which themselves beg many questions. Equally important would be the aesthetic and symbolic strategies in terms of which the potencies of tradition are indeed actualized. When one transposes the inquiry from Germany to this country one can, however, recognize areas of critical attention to my brother's work which could well be pursued. Certainly one of these would be a sympathetic study of his public, and the role played in the response to his novels and plays of what Oppel speaks of as the "audience psychology and apperception mass" of those elements in the American population. Perhaps, if much criticism has not known what to do with this author or how to locate him, it is because it has not known how to come to terms with our larger American reality.

If we speak of audience psychology or the relation of an artist to his public, having in mind the situation of an American writer in our period, we are of course confronted with difficult and controversial issues. If we recognize the importance of the symbolics and answering imagination of a society or of groups within that society as bearing on the resonance of the work of a given author, we still have problems of criteria and discrimination. The sociology of literary taste is all too aware of the mediocrity and provincialism which can determine the acoustics of large elements of the public in their encounter with the arts. But in an epoch like ours there can also be the mistake of narrowing the purview and losing sight of the wider vitalities and registers of response in the society.

All this is only to suggest that there is still much unfinished business for the American critic with reference to a writer like my brother. His popularity, the links hidden and overt between his vision and the expectations of this New-World breed, should not forthwith be construed as suspect. What is called for is a sophisticated discrimination, both aesthetic and sociological, of our American reality, its symbolism and dynamics, its peculiar creative modes and registers of meaning. Related to these will be distinctive and recurrent expressive patterns, styles, scenarios, genres, *topoi;* in short, modes of language and fabulation which, as in the structural study of a tribe, reflect the basic orientation.

With such an approach, again, an inclusive critical method would not look on what it sees as the moral and metaphysical aspects of a writer's work as out of bounds, but as inseparable dimensions of any work of art oriented to the deeper apperception of a society.

There is a curious imbalance in a great deal of modern criticism. It is highly sophisticated about genetic and cultural factors in the arts of our most alienated and deracinated circles. This kind of aesthetic probing appears to be arrested and is not exercised when it confronts the imaginative legacies and repertoire of the many.

An index of this anomaly is the lengths to which such critics will go to expropriate such figures as Emerson and Walt Whitman as fathers and precursors of the modern writers they prize. No doubt lines can be drawn from such American classics to a poet like Wallace Stevens, but their essential legacy is surely to be found elsewhere in the wider creativity of our society.

These observations have their bearing on one feature of my essay, its occasional polemic strain. Appreciation of my brother's writing in various critical quarters has inevitably been conditioned by the reigning canons of the period, shaped as these have been by great models and liberators and related to worldwide cultural factors. Such criteria rightly orient our assessment of the arts of our time. But here qualifications are in order. In lesser hands these emancipations and norms have tended to become narrow and dogmatic. Ideological alignments

intrude. Critical schools with particular aesthetic or cultural commitments forfeit awareness of a more total reality and its imaginative
transcription. Modernism can have its own chapels of vested interest,
its own defensive moralities, and its own parochialism. Fortunately
there are always those wider observers in every generation who stand
above the local engagements and appeal to a more universal tradition.
Indeed, the dilemma, the unsolved question, of modernism from the
time of its pioneers on, and including what we call "the modern
classics," has always been that of continuity with the past. As its once
essential iconoclasm today begins to forfeit substance, the task of
retrieval not only of the past but of a more total human experience
becomes mandatory.

Here an observation by Bertrand Poirot-Delpech is very much to
the point. Reviewing Octavio Paz's book, *Pointe de convergence,* in
Le Monde, under the caption, "Fin de l'art moderne," he writes:

> The aesthetics of change which has held sway for a good century and a
> half will show itself as illusory as the imitation of the ancients. The age
> now beginning will scrutinize the changeless principles of all art, the
> basis common to the *Odyssey* and to Proust.*

That the arts of our climate and their criticism should reflect the
exceptional features of our modern crisis is all to their credit, and all
the more so when we recognize the full gamut and depth of the
transformations in course. It is understandable, therefore, that the
modern intellectual and artist should be captivated by this experience, these tasks, and by the special awarenesses and sensibility
so mediated. But the human story transcends even such convulsive
vicissitudes, and both the thinker and the artist are condemned to
myopia if they take their bearings only from the immediate occasion,
however absorbing.

In dedicating this book to my sister Isabel I would like to convey
some sense of the immeasurable service she rendered to our brother
through the years. At the time of his first successes, in the situation of

---

*Le Monde Hebdomadaire, No. 1428 (4-10 Mars, 1976), p. 12.

the family, willy-nilly, as a kind of Johnny-on-the-spot, thanks to her talents and training, she became an indispensable aid to him in many particulars and relationships. Through the decades she was inescapably involved in his career—professionally with respect to his publications, productions, and appointments, and personally with respect to the literary and dramatic circles in which he moved both at home and abroad. It was not only her own initiation as a writer and her schooling in the theater which thus qualified her but above all her universally recognized warmth of spirit, vivacity, and fortitude, which indeed only represented another version of the same traits in Thornton himself.

Blue Hill Falls, Maine   Amos N. Wilder
June 1979.

ACKNOWLEDGMENTS

An article based on this book was published in *Literaturwissenschaftliches Jahrbuch* (Berlin) XX (1979) with the title, "He Didn't Go to Paris: Thornton Wilder, Middle America and the Critics." I wish to express my appreciation to Franz H. Link who was associate editor of this issue of the annual.

I wish also to register my appreciation to Donald Gallup, Curator of the Thornton Wilder Collection in the Beinecke Library at Yale; to my sister Isabel Wilder and to Wilhelm Pauck for their letters quoted; to my wife Catharine and our children, as well as my sister, Janet Dakin, for their promptings and suggestions; and to Norman and Ingalill Hjelm for their personal interest and resourceful assistance at various stages of the publication of this book.

THORNTON WILDER
AND
HIS PUBLIC

There is a greater analogy between the instinctive life of the wider public and the talent of a great writer...than in the superficial verbiage and the changing criteria of the official judges.[1]
> — *Marcel Proust*

NOW FOR SOME TIME the critics by and large have not been able to fit the novels and plays of Thornton Wilder into their picture of modern writing and its agenda. They evidently have some qualms about this, since his work was so innovative and versatile and has had so profound a resonance in a wide public both at home and abroad. Yet there is a certain traditionalism in his outlook which undermines the modern premise. In his best-known plays and in much of his fiction he appears to speak for a grass-roots American experience which they may look on as banal, insipid, or moralistic. But what if his "notation of the heart" is, indeed, that of Mr. and Mrs. Antrobus, that is, Everyman? And what if his inquisition goes beneath the sentiment of Grover's Corners or the Philistinism of Coaltown, Illinois, to some deeper human marrow?

It is a question of the anonymous millions in our streets and countryside, and of finding a register and a language for their potential. In 1957 Wilder spoke on "Culture in a Democracy" to a German audience in Frankfurt at the award of the Peace Prize of the German publishers.[2] He took as his text a shocking passage from Walt Whitman: Is there one of the great classics of the ancients or of Europe "that is consistent with these United States...or whose underlying basis is not a denial and insult to democracy?" He went on to speak of the dangers but also of the "unknown factors" and the "promise" of an enfranchised society of equals of the kind which Whitman had envisaged. This kind of passionate empathy for Grover's Corners or Main Street — both magnanimous and austere — is too often missing in our modern classics and our critics of culture. The response to

[1] *A la recherche du temps perdu* (Pléiade edn., vol. III). Paris, 1957. pp. 893–894.

[2] *Kultur in einer Demokratie*. Frankfurt, 1957. For the English text of this address see Supplement below, pp. 93–98.

27

change and its advocacy takes precedence over the deeper human continuities.

<h1 style="text-align:center">I</h1>

Critics and critical schools in this country have understandably been suspicious of writers who have had large popular success. They have been baffled by any conjunction of true excellence with midbrow or lowbrow appeal as registered in the categories of "best-seller" or "book-club" selection. In the case of Wilder there has been a long history of embarrassment if not attack, and even of assignment to limbo. One can recall disparagement of the first three novels as effete or precious; Blackmur's dissatisfaction with *Heaven's My Destination* as aimed at the book clubs; the critics' "snubbing" of *The Ides of March*; more recently, dismissal by Stanley Kauffmann and others of *The Eighth Day* as a sermon or an exercise in old clichés.

As for the plays, while they are continually being staged at the grass-roots level throughout the country, any more ambitious revival is likely to meet the critical incomprehension which recently greeted *The Skin of Our Teeth* in its Bicentennial presentation in New York.

For awareness of this dilemma one can cite a review in the London *Times Literary Supplement* of Wilder's last novel, *Theophilus North*.

> In a literary career spanning half a century, Thornton Wilder has successfully resisted any kind of classification as novelist or playwright. We cannot pin him down, as we can Hemingway or Scott Fitzgerald, to background or subject matter (though both his first and his latest books are almost entirely autobiographical), and it is impossible to group him conveniently with any coterie of writers, whether prewar or postwar. Popularity and success — implicit in the huge sales (10,000 copies a week) of *The Bridge of San Luis Rey* — may have dented his reputation a little among those for whom starving in a garret is the sole criterion of artistic excellence. How, on the other hand, are we to account for the fact that in several European countries Mr. Wilder, along with Shakespeare and Joyce, is one of a mere handful of English-speaking writers known to the reading public?[3]

[3] July 12, 1974.

Yet many accomplished critics by now have their minds made up. Wilder, they agree, is indeed somewhat anomalous and hard to pigeonhole, but he falls outside the main line of advance of the novel or the drama. His work has been on the margin of those explorations and engagements so essential to our twentieth-century experience. Worst of all, he smacks of Middle America and even a disguised religiosity. Thus all across the board — subject matter, outlook, style — he does not fit the common premise or lend himself to the central debate.

In seeking to identify the reservations of the critics we can at least set aside some of the earlier imputations. Literary judges have long disallowed partisan Marxist charges made against him in the thirties, even if changing categories of social realism and relevance may still be invoked. *Our Town* is no longer banned in the U.S.S.R. despite its alleged complaisance with the bourgeois family. *The Skin of Our Teeth* is similarly permitted there, though formerly excluded on the ground that wars and other calamities are not attributed in it to capitalist exploitation.

Critics have also now long dropped the charge of plagiarism against one of James Joyce's most revering excavators and glossators. Wilder happily conceded that, like some irreproachable predecessors, if he was a shoplifter he always preyed upon the best emporia. As Emerson remarks in his essay on Shakespeare, "Thought is the property of him who can entertain it and of him who can adequately place it."

The reservations of the critics today have other grounds. Their disparagement, neglect, or bracketing of Wilder's work is not necessarily to be put down to the insensitivity of reviewers or to critical fashion and partisanship. The situation is much more interesting than that. As I have suggested, it comes down to the basic premise with regard to modern letters. One must beg the original question. Where, indeed, does the main engagement lie in our modern situation? Granted that "modernism" has had a great and necessary task of liberation to carry out in our epoch, what may have been left out in its view of that task and its engagement with our contemporary reality?

Are not the options, strategies, and agenda of modern letters richer than those envisaged in even the best critical orthodoxy of the time? Has it been as responsive to ancient wisdoms and to what David Jones called the "deposits," the "fertile ashes," the *anathémata* of the long past as it has to our modern experience? Has it been nourished by the inchoate impulses, the stifled myth, of the many as well as by the changing sensibility of the elites and the articulate?

The modern focus has understandably been one of revolt and emancipation, and Thornton Wilder has not been a stranger to it. But there should always be those who speak for the deeper ground which continues through change. Perhaps artists of this kind fall through the net of the existing tribunals. While the instinctive response of the wider public recognizes them, the official judges are at a loss.

When one moves the question to the American scene the issues become clearer. How do we define the "modern" here, and what is the relation of its proper iconoclasm to our older American heritage? It is a question of locating the deeper potential and the hidden springs of our many-layered society. One premise is that the clue and norm for us runs from the expatriates after World War I down through those writers who have extricated themselves not only from an earlier "genteel" tradition but from any rootage in what seem the blinkered pieties and conformisms of an older America.

It is true that many of our best writers have rightly been in revolt against Philistinism and inhumanity in our folkways. In aesthetic terms they have rightly sought a new language and new vehicles for a new sensibility. But, along with the critics, have they not also scanted the depths of our people and left a great deal of unfinished business? The fertility of the New World has always thrown up its own original and even plebeian celebrations, versions of its own native mythology. Here is one point at which Thornton Wilder comes in.

Nothing is more revealing of critical myopia than assignment of Wilder to the category of "midcult." Granted that this is a step up from "masscult," it still connotes ingratiation of a Philistine public. But is the general public so obtuse and so negligible? This kind of classification makes things too easy for the critic. It is his task to distinguish between the wheat and the straw, and not only between the modern and the traditional. Just as there is a great deal of the new which is

mainly imitative and of mediocre talent, so there is much of the
seeming traditional which is highly creative in its own context and
horizon. But the category of midcult sweeps both the saccharine and
the profoundly disciplined into one common basket. One recalls how
grudgingly many critics came to concede the merits of Robert Frost.

Even more shallow is the implied judgment on the wider public.
There are in our population various kinds of literacy and illiteracy,
various registers and acoustics for the arts and the imagination. No
doubt there is much of the moronic, the sentimental, and the crass.
These exhibit themselves also in many of our iconoclastic novelties.
But the great continental public "out there," seemingly regressive
and insensitive, is highly complex and unpredictable. No one dogma
or program of the aesthetic should pretend to arbitrate for so rich and
incalculable a gestation.

In any society, granted a wide mediocrity, if there is a valid
pioneering elite of artists and intellectuals, there is also a diffused and
unrecognized remnant which bears the heritage of the many and its
costs and its promise. However scornful the elite may be of Main
Street and suburbia, it should not cut itself off from the voices that
witness through the shapeless and the inarticulate.

In assigning Wilder to midcult, certain critics identify his work
with cliché, banality, and indulgence. But this is to overlook certain
highly rigorous aspects of his work. Such glossy or superficial writings as can properly be assigned to this category rest, for example, on
no such extensive literacy as that of my brother, no such intimacy
with the great models and their exacting demands. Whatever read-
ability for a general public his books possess, this simplicity or wide
appeal rests on an immense repertoire of aesthetic and intellectual
tuition, which is, as it were, distilled in them. The ambiance of his
thought, his mental climate or *habitus* was that of the masters, and
there is no greater achievement of the "art of the difficult" than that
of simplicity, if that is the word for it.

I can suggest the range of this American writer's acquaintance with
the world of letters by offering a few examples. His familiarity with
the Greek and Roman classics is evident in much of his writing. This
goes back especially to the year he spent after his graduation from

Yale at the American Academy in Rome. It was especially on classical epic and drama that he lectured during numerous summer terms
at the University of Chicago. Classicists will appreciate the significance of the close friendship and animated conversation he carried on
over a period with the great scholar Karl Reinhardt, discussions
that bore not only on the Greek tragedians but also on such German
poets as Hölderlin.

As for Romance languages his early stylistic ''crush'' on Mme. de
Sévigné carried over, of course, to *The Bridge of San Luis Rey,* in
which the letters of the Marquesa de Montemayor to her daughter
echo the pattern. Thornton's M.A. degree at Princeton was in French
under Professor Louis Cons, and his earliest teaching, at the Law-
renceville School, was in this department. Later, one of his longtime
distractions, as a problem in literary detection, was the dating of the
plays of the Spanish dramatist, Lope de Vega, a topic on which he
wrote a paper for the Modern Language Association. He enjoyed his
correspondence with the leading Spanish authority on this intricate
topic, as he did his correspondence with Walter Lowrie about Kierkegaard, to whose work Lowrie had introduced him when they were
both in Rome where the former was rector of the American church,
St. Paul's.

Another picture-puzzle passion of Thornton's for years was his
annotation of *Finnegans Wake,* the decoding of which inevitably
required a large fund of linguistic and literary resource. In a quite
different sector Thornton also followed with close attention the publication of the many volumes of the Yale Edition of *Horace Walpole's
Correspondence,* edited by his friend and former schoolmate, Wilmarth Lewis. The latter has testified to the helpfulness of my brother's
many letters about Walpole and the acuteness of his observations.
They both had been introduced to the writers of this period by the
great Chauncey Tinker at Yale.

I refer at a later point to Thornton's acquaintance with Goethe and
other German writers and the opening this afforded him especially to
circles of German students in his visits to that country. Other areas of
literary initiation could be cited, not least the American classics on
which he lectured at Harvard. Yet though he was in so many respects

a polymath, in his own writing he availed himself of all such resources in his own sovereign way.

In categorizing his role as an American writer this broad literary
culture should be kept in mind. It was this range of his literacy which
explains the mutual cordiality and correspondence between him and
Edmund Wilson. Both were "men of letters" in the European sense.
With this kind of tuition Thornton's art, however accessible to a wide
public, could never be popular in a disparaging sense. Nor should his
academic associations be viewed as suspect since his humanism was
as deep as it was wide.

Assessment of my brother's contribution in the long run will need
to take account of more than his few novels and plays. Their resonance can be trivialized if seen out of context. In this case the author's
life and work were interwoven, and one illuminates the other. There
are writers best known for a few works who, nevertheless, constitute
one kind of "presence" in their period, one kind of option or index or
even synthesis in their times. Their writings can have a kind of
divinatory impact related to the cultural scene, and this is related to
their personal history and involvements. What Thornton Wilder represented in terms of cultural ripeness and mastery — as teacher, figure
in world letters, correspondent, idea man and conversationalist — all
this reflects itself in his formal writings, and vice versa. Just as in his
plays, so in his quicksilver-like talk, whether at the Algonquin Hotel
or in a P. E. N. session abroad or a college common room or a bar, he
brought worlds together and sparkled with searching insights.

Commentators have, indeed, been puzzled by the fact that he wrote
so little and by those intervals in his career in which he did not seem to
be productive. Even the wider public had heard of projects which he
did not complete such as the Kafka-like play to be called *The Empor-
ium* or the cycles of one-act plays devoted to the seven ages of man
and to the seven deadly sins, both series evidencing his interest in
modernizing the old "morality" genre typified by *Everyman*. It was
suggested that he too easily allowed himself to be diverted by academic appointments or cultural missions, or even by war service.

It is true that he could joke about a proposed epitaph: "Here lies a
man who tried to be obliging." Annals of his residence terms in

Burton-Goodspeed Hall at the University of Chicago and in Harvard's Dunster House evoke the protracted meal times and midnight sorties with students, the fledgling manuscripts read, the many speaking appointments accepted, and the personal crises of youth for which he was so skillful and austere an analyst. There were wider calls he could not refuse: an unexpected additional course at Harvard; some Broadway production of a friend calling for a translation from the French, or requiring surgery; a plea from Alfred Hitchcock and Hollywood.

But this artist's role included all such gregariousness, involvement, pedagogy, and missions. His private fabulation carried over into all such public and oral occasions. His theater carried over into daily life. His formal works are related to this wider deportment as sage, mage, democrat, and soldier. He liked to act in his own plays. There was something of the histrionic in all he did. When he lectured he was all over the platform and down the aisles, gesturing, challenging, clowning, and taking the parts of the characters discussed. So it was also with his talk on more intimate occasions. His gusto and affections evoked scenarios ''as good as a play.''

With some authors, life is one thing and literature another. When this observation was made to Edmund Wilson he replied: ''But isn't literature simply a part of life as much as conversation?'' In the case of my brother, at least, this is highly pertinent. Like his conversation –understood either as his talk or in the old biblical sense of his deportment or way in the world–his novels and plays were gestures or overflow of his life. I cannot therefore deplore that he spent himself in so many other theaters at the expense of his writing.

In retrospect, what may well deserve attention in the cultural history of our period will be Wilder as a distinctive type and product of our American society. His formal works will only be part of the total image. No doubt other authors will be credited with greater achievement in their own kind. Other novelists and playwrights will be identified with crucial movements in the age. But at the level where American roots are linked with modern sophistication, and where American moralities are linked critically and imaginatively with old-world legacies, there have been fewer witnesses in our time.

No doubt humanist scholars have sought to bridge these gaps. But what is more difficult, yet essential, is that these poles should be linked in art and poetry.

One test of this scope and role is afforded by international cultural encounters. On certain occasions when meetings were held abroad under such auspices as UNESCO it was difficult to find American delegates who were not only scholars familiar with European literature past and present, but also and at the same time creative artists whose work was appreciated abroad. That Wilder could fill this double role and share in discussions in several languages meant a unique kind of American participation in Western culture. The same kind of total humanistic outreach was exhibited in the Goethe Festival at Aspen in 1949 when, as I detail further in what follows, my brother found himself called on to assist on the platform with the translation of the addresses of Albert Schweitzer on one day and of Ortega y Gasset on the next.

I have been illustrating my brother's extensive acquaintance with the world of letters as one answer to the charge of banality or indulgence in his writing. But rigor rather than indulgence appears also in the ethos of his work. If there is, indeed, a large charity in his portrayal of life and much gaiety, yet no one should miss the uncompromising severity that accompanies these. There was iron in his outlook, some combination perhaps of granite from Calvin and worldly wisdom from his cherished Goethe. We can recognize it not only in the austere Caesar of *The Ides of March* but also in the disabused acidity that runs through *The Skin of Our Teeth*. The unmasking of human motivation associated with modern thought was taken up by him into a more radical suspicion. But it did not leave him in the condition of so many who are tempted to cynicism, or who have nothing but pathos to fall back on with respect to their heroes or anti-heroes. This combination of generosity of spirit with austerity is far from sentimentality, but equally uncongenial to many moderns.

Even in the first year of his exposure to Europe and his ravishment by its high culture, when in Italy he was piecing together his most fastidious novel, *The Cabala* (at one time to be called *Romans*), he writes in a letter home: "A horror grows on me for the purely aesthetic; I am fierce for the strange, the strong, the remorseless; even the brutal and the coarse. The vivid and the significant; not the graceful."

II

The following reflections combine literary observations with a certain amount of biographical data about my brother and family history, and the latter aspect calls for some prefatory explanation. What may seem a gratuitous input of private matter may in this case have some justification. The annals and vicissitudes of our family have their transmuted echoes in his writing, and at various levels. The review in question is very much to the point if it helps to identify the matrix of his own personal vision and his view of the American writer.

Critical assessment or disparagement of Wilder's work is often explicitly or implicitly related to his kind of family background and to what many today see as an addiction to outworn cultural patterns and literary styles. It may be a question, however, of what kind of tradition was operative, and of the ability to recognize its continuing cultural vitality. Thus the suspect traditionalism or paideia of a writer like my brother is not too hastily to be deprecated. Evidently a basic issue as to the true locus and meaning of the American heritage is raised. Some review, therefore, of the formative factors in his development should illuminate the wider options.

The recurrent epithet in characterizations of my brother's family background is that it was Puritan or Calvinist, and this is often taken as answering many questions about his work. The several manuals about him commonly include a short account of his childhood and education. His parents were "very religious"; his father was a reformer and disciplinarian; he went to missionary schools in China; he was sent to Oberlin, a college with a devout tradition, before transferring to Yale. His early one-act plays, many of which (like his first full-length play, *The Trumpet Shall Sound*) were written when he was an undergraduate, show his liking for biblical texts.

The rehearsal of these matters can then lead to the simplistic view that Wilder's later work was shaped by these influences to a blandly affirmative view of life. Or it can be deduced that his upbringing sheltered him from exposure to the real world with which modern letters should deal. Not only that, but to the handicaps of a pious formation was added the later buffer of long academic association. In short, he was never deeply initiated into the modern situation; "he did not go to Paris" with the expatriates, and was not involved overseas in World War I. He was therefore never fully disabused of Victorian and bourgeois illusions just as he was disqualified by a religious hangover from that necessary, searing experience of modern alienation which is an essential premise of the modern artist.

As a parenthesis here I cannot resist interjecting one observation, by way of anticipation. As his personal correspondence over the years shows, my brother was wholly conversant and profoundly sympathetic with the great iconoclasts of our epoch, their revulsions and their works, whether discursive or literary. Both his letters and his conversation registered delighted encounters with such figures as Freud and Sartre and searching appreciation of their thought. If his sense for the modern departed from that of the reigning ideologies and the arts associated with them, it was not because he fell short of their experience and grasp but because he appropriated them to his own purposes. One citation from his letters is illustrative.

In the student protest at the University of Genoa I saw the slogan many times repeated

MARX   MAO   MARCUSE

I've been reading Marcuse; lots of sharp diagnoses. The students know that he's just as harsh on Kremlin corruption as he is on the Western total authority. The Technological Society is soothingly, blandly reducing man to one-dimensional being–and the universities are instruments of this new enslavement. He's very drastic on the image of the erotic that is being imposed. Imperial Rome said "give them bread and circuses to keep them nerveless"–and the New Society says give them sexual permissiveness–"the opiate of the masses!" The word is *de-sublimation*. Very perceptive.

But he can't describe the poly-dimensional man. Neither could Nietzsche–neither can Sartre.

Thornton Wilder was no stranger to the anomie of our epoch. And just as he was intimate over long periods of immersion in the works of Kafka, Joyce, Proust, Broch, Stein, and other modern masters, so he was at home with the great pioneers and iconoclasts of modern thought and with the master texts and pamphlets of the time. Just as his earlier correspondence echoed his attention to Kierkegaard, Spengler, Lukács, and Valéry, so his later letters show him absorbed in the successive volumes of Lévi-Strauss. It should be clear from this review that he was no outsider to the cultural and aesthetic dislocations of our period or the great debates which have accompanied them. Whatever ''Puritan'' or ''academic'' or ''classicist'' liabilities may be charged against him and against his family background, these do not appear to have isolated him from the main currents of the age. Quite the converse, they may rather have endowed him with a deeper human orientation that could assimilate the new experience in a more universal vision.

My main plea will have to do with my brother's Americanism and his probing of the common stuff of American life in which certain religious ingredients are to be recognized. Herman Melville related Hawthorne's moral and spiritual view of man to, what Melville called, ''that unshackled democratic spirit of Christianity in all things.'' In his *American Renaissance* F.O. Matthiessen finds this same vision in Melville himself and the phrase takes on large importance in Matthiessen's own total survey and personal orientation.[4]

Since I am concerned with my brother's work in this context, it is necessary here to recall some familiar issues about American culture in our period and the options and resources of our writers. Despite the erosion of older patterns we still have to reckon with the formative factors, the basic mythology of the country, and the religious quotient in our usable past.

One can side with those historians who assign priority to the legacy of the Enlightenment. Or, as with such recent studies as those of Sydney Ahlstrom and Robert Bellah, one can locate the dominant vision in the mutations of the Calvinist tradition. In any case the wide

---

[4]Giles B. Gunn, *F.O. Matthiessen: The Critical Achievement*, Seattle and London. 1975, pp. 107, 125–126.

diffusion of the biblical-Puritan archetypes through our society is recognized, for better or worse, and despite whatever pluralism or secularization. This is what is pointed to in the characterization of the United States as a nation "with the soul of a church," or in speaking of the "civil religion" of the American people.

Even if one preferred otherwise, this quasi-theocratic paradigm is so deeply implanted and so recurrently manifest in many strata of our population that our fabulists and image makers must take account of it. Of course there are many valid special domains of the arts which need not engage these roots. There are also important cultural communities and Bohemias whose aesthetic is determined by cosmopolitan models and ideologies. No doubt, on this last point, the New World shares in the fate of the West. But whatever revolutions of images and sensibility may have been achieved abroad must be sifted and transformed if they are to be domesticated in our climate.

It is readily to be admitted that our peculiar moral and metaphysical legacies have long been interwoven with Philistinism in our culture and inhumanity in our mores. One can therefore appreciate the fact that a main task of modernism in our period, both in criticism and in the arts, has been to challenge these legacies and to dismantle the tradition. In writing on Faulkner I have stressed his concern with "vestigial moralities" and "otiose codes," and recognized that just as there can be a Southern way of life which nourishes and one that strangles, so there can be a Puritan granite which strengthens and one that crushes.

But there remains nonetheless the deeper question as to the springs of our common life and the residual archetypes. However misconstrued and betrayed they may have been in the sequel, the basic covenants of our society still operate, the ground of those "still undiminished resources" which Matthiessen affirmed, echoing the promise which he found in his study of our classical American writers. In view of the pervasiveness and stubborn hold of these legacies, neither our politics nor our arts can long ignore them.

This situation has a number of corollaries for the writer in this country. As indicated, modernism with all its various lineages and vicissitudes, and despite its surpassing achievements, emerged in a European setting and, as an essentially imported phenomenon, has never fully related to our American reality. The expatriate tradition and its liberating models have had an invaluable catalytic impact on the American imagination but the hiatus remains.

The American experience resists certain old-world categories and scenarios. The clearest recalcitrance arising out of our native vision goes back to our social archetype. It has been observed that the deepest myth that is gestating in the New World is of the political order. Whether our saga speak of democracy, the American dream, or the Kingdom of God in America, and however we may deflate these, our instincts as a people and our emblems and rituals point to a new kind of commonweal or social compact. Through all its vicissitudes its antecedents lie in the biblical and Latin models of the founders.

This social dream is uncongenial to those iconoclasms understandable in the European situation, which have played such a large part in modern letters. Cultural factors on the Continent determined distinctive forms of revolt over generations which in the field of the arts account for much of what has been identified as "modern" and "avant-garde." In this country the problem of authority and liberation has been a different one. On the Continent the break with the past was necessarily more radical.

The outcome has been specially clear in the trend toward subjectivism and psychologism. In her book, *Against Interpretation*, Susan Sontag observes that "modern man lives with an increasing burden of subjectivity; at the expense of his sense of the reality of the world." This has special relevance to the modern sensibility as it has developed abroad. No doubt significant elements in our society shared in the modern experience of alienation. But with a difference.

In Germany, Kantian and neo-Kantian influences; in France, symbolism, Romantic and neo-Romantic impulses: both lines furthered this loss of the sense of the reality of the world, and especially of life's social dimension. In addition, the class structure of Europe meant that the creative movements of the elites were not deeply nourished by the residual legacies of the many. Thus, while the great authors of what we call the modern classics wrestled with the problem of order, they did so on terms very different from those of our own tradition.

In the cultural quandary and distractions of our own situation here in America signs have not been wanting of a renewed exploration of our own peculiar givens and our native mythology. Deeper than literary regionalism, pietist revivals, or our recent Bicentennial rituals, one can recognize an impulse to reclaim what was authentic in the promise of the New World, a nostalgia coming to expression in writers and artists whom none can accuse of chauvinism.

For an example all the more significant because of his own modernist sympathies, one can cite a poem of Delmore Schwartz, in which he speaks of

> A fabulous discovery of America, of the opulence
>   hidden in the dark depths and glittering
>   heights of reality.

The poem, "Once and for All,"[5] represents a kind of spiritual autobiography. The poet's imagination had been enthralled first by Apollo and later by Dionysus. He learns that he had been wrong in both of these soul dramas of an elder world, whether dreams of innocence or cyclic rehearsals of death and rebirth.

> and when I knew how I was wrong I knew
> What, in a way, I had known all along:
> This was the new world, here I
>   belonged, here I was wrong because
> Here every tragedy has a happy
>   ending, and any error may be
> A fabulous discovery of America . . .

What he means by the old options now surmounted is even more clearly stated in his poem, "The True-Blue American":[6]

[5]Selected Poems: *Summer Knowledge*, New York, 1957, p. 222.
[6]*Ibid.*, pp. 163–164.

Rejecting the either-or of Kierkegaard, and many another European;
Refusing to accept alternatives, refusing to believe the
   choice of between;
Rejecting selection; denying dilemma; electing absolute
   affirmation: knowing
      in his breast
         The infinite and the gold
         Of the endless frontier, the deathless West.

The poem ends, speaking of the true-blue American boy, Jeremiah
Dickson:

      Taught by Christmas, by the circus, by the vulgarity
         and grandeur of
            Niagara Falls and the Grand Canyon,
      Tutored by the grandeur, vulgarity, and infinite
         appetite gratified and
            Shining in the darkness, of the light
      On Saturdays at the double bills of the moon pictures,
      The consummation of the advertisements of the
         imagination of the light
      Which is as it was — the infinite belief in infinite
         hope — of Columbus,
            Barnum, Edison, and Jeremiah Dickson.

   This kind of revisualizing of the spiritual options of the modern
world and its mythologies, the options of Nietzsche ''and many
another European'' — a revisualizing anticipated indeed in William
Blake's auguries of America — points to the deepest strata in our
national consciousness. Other writers may invoke more particular
motifs of the religious and social perspectives of the founders. But all
such imaginative exploration of our own tribal myth and roots should
have high priority. The best way to overcome betrayals of the American dream is to mine it for its deeper yield and to celebrate its
unpredictable outcomes. For these tasks many familiar critical and
artistic strategies are unsuited.

I have introduced these larger considerations about our society in order to clarify some important aspects of my brother's writing. Significant works of the imagination require and make their appeal to some shared cultural experience and registers of response. It is a question of acoustics. No doubt there are diverse elements and layers in our population resonating to diverse signals. As there are wide differences in apperception and sensibility, so the arts thus variously conditioned will differ.

Granted this diversity, some special importance should be assigned to those arts which sound the deeper common registers of our American reality. Whether we speak of the American dream or, in structuralist terms, of a "deep structure" of imagery beneath all our social forms, we should recognize this order of acoustics and communication. In our society as in others there are sounding boards which can be struck, inflammable deposits which can be ignited. Here in the public imagination are ultimate sources of creativity as well as the norms of a truer self-awareness.

Nor need such exploitation of our special American givens be construed as parochial. Just as it is pursued in the light of other cultural quests, so it shares in a global exchange of shock and response. But those distinctive rhetorics and scenarios which trace to our own baptism as a people and to our own saga should not be disowned. One can find an example, indeed, of this kind of profitable exchange in the work of Matthiessen to which I have referred. In the closing section of *American Renaissance* and in other writings, the continuing legacy of our own moral and spiritual vision as a people is brought to bear as a test on such more recent writers as Henry James, Eliot, and Yeats. As I shall have occasion to note at a later point, it was those plays and utterances in which Thornton Wilder evoked most deeply our own folk pieties and promise which found an answering imagination abroad, receiving their widest echo in a shattered Germany and Central Europe.

If Wilder's work is seen as shaped by religious influences, or viewed as unmodern for that reason, it can hardly be because he orchestrates specific tenets or rites of a churchly tradition. After his earliest plays any explicit biblical or devout thematic appears only in a highly eclectic and oblique form. The representation of the afterlife in the closing scene of *Our Town* can appear heretical to the theologian. In *The Skin of Our Teeth* Mr. Antrobus is as concerned to save Homer and the Muses as he is Moses. The Caesar of *The Ides of March* is transparently attacking the opiates and enervations of religious custom today in his recurrent disquisitions on the Roman ceremonies.

One has to go back to *The Woman of Andros* to find a fable pointing at all directly to the Christian dispensation, and here only in the first and last paragraphs of the book with its reference to the land, which was later to be called holy and which was even then "preparing its precious burden." Like its model by Cervantes, Wilder's *Heaven's My Destination* is as much a satire on its Christian tradition as a celebration of it.

Apart from such ambiguous motifs, avant-garde critics have found other grounds for charges of didacticism in the writings. Bourgeois values appear to be exalted in "The Long Christmas Dinner" and in *Our Town*. The hero of *The Eighth Day* can rightly be viewed as a Kierkegaardian Knight of Faith. But Kierkegaard's point about this kind of hero is that he is unrecognizable as such and does not even know his own merit. Thornton told me that the several sections of *Theophilus North* represent studies of different kinds of love. Indeed, themes of the three virtues, faith, hope, and charity, are recurrent in the writings. But in every instance the objector should pay heed to the total aesthetic plot or fable in which they are found. At this properly artistic level strictures will go back to fundamental differences of assumption and horizon.

The important question, finally, with respect to all such imaginative works is that of their scale and of the moral theater to which they appeal. This bears both on their aesthetic and their human stature. Whatever particular settings or culturally determined motifs a writer may employ, what is ultimately determinative is the basic vision or orientation of his art and the range of its resonance. In this context the deeper story or activating myth in my brother's fictions rejoins the American dream both with respect to its humanism and its austere biblical antecedents.

Whatever other special veins other contemporary artists may exploit, or whatever aesthetic strategies they may pursue, it is essential that some should wrestle with our ultimate pieties at the plebeian level, blocked as they may be, with some sense of their vivacious and unpredictable potential.

This is only to continue that focus on the common man or woman, the anonymous American, celebrated by Whitman and Melville, that "untamed breed," in Perry Miller's characterization — recalling Emerson's declaration in "The American Scholar" that "not only out of those on whom systems of education have exhausted their culture, comes the helpful giant to destroy the old or to build the new but out of unhandselled savage nature."

But this particular breed, the American Adam, has not issued from nature unshaped by his own historical baptism and predestination. These formative factors and the pervasiveness of their symbolism should not be lost sight of by poet and fabulist since they condition the health and cultural fertility of this human type.

III

The foregoing considerations have a bearing on any supposed handicaps of my brother's nurture and outlook. What may appear as a liability in his Puritan indebtedness may rather have been an asset. It is a question not only of his own horizons as a modern writer but of his public. What I have said about the new mold of man in the New World and his legacies suggests that there can be wide miscalculations as to the American audience. In dismissing as infertile or banal large elements of our society, the artist and the critic may overlook the deeper root systems of the common life and their creative promise.

I return now, however, to the topic of my brother's family background and training. As I have noted, some rehearsal of these personal matters can be illuminating with respect both to his view of the American writer and to the writings themselves. There are, moreover, recurrent errors and misjudgments about his family and early years which need to be corrected. More importantly, there is a wide inability in many circles today to appreciate the kind of distinctive strain in our society here represented. These matters can only be put in their right light if I go into certain aspects of the family history at some length. Particular details of it will also furnish occasion for related observations about Thornton's later and wider experience and achievements.

In this review it is inevitable that I should give special attention to the role of our father in my brother's development. Again the twofold reason for my chronicle applies: to set the record straight, and to fill in the picture of one kind of American tradition. This parent of Maine background had certain of the robust and granitic traits and that "interfering spirit of righteousness" associated with the Calvinist heritage, a type widely derided today. My brother had his troubles with him, and one can find a disquisition on father-son relations included in Thornton's Frankfurt address already mentioned, apropos of hierarchic patterns abroad. But the paradox in this case was that this same overshadowing father was also the one who imbued my brother with his deepest insights into American grass-roots values and their hidden operations. This needs to be spelled out in detail. Indeed, I am tempted here to apply Samson's riddle, "Out of the strong came forth sweetness," as a parable of the ultimate relation of Puritanism to the arts: out of the lion came forth honey.

In referring to Wilder's early years biographers are content to characterize his father as a forbidding Calvinist type, and it is implied that he was disposed to stifle aesthetic aspirations in his children. Implicitly or explicitly it is suggested that he thwarted my brother's development. With the contemporary vogue of psychobiography this opens the way to freewheeling analysis. Familiar schemata can be imposed on the father-son relationship which then supposedly account for what are seen as limitations in the latter's art.

In any case, given the family background, the assumption can be encouraged that the author of *Our Town* was so conditioned that he was never able to make a clean break with the enervating influence of a didactic, ascetic, and moralistic rearing. His seeming complaisance with dated family values, as reflected in his work; his espousal of the hopes of at least an underground remnant in our society; his focus on a dimension of wrestling and survival deeper even than that of contemporary alienation — all this can be seen as evidence of a crippling anachronism. A writer with such nostalgias must be viewed as one tied to an older and irrelevant outlook.

In what follows I am concerned to balance and correct the stereotyped picture of our father so recurrently evoked. But my main object is to trace major features of my brother's accomplishment to the kind of values and the kind of Americanism represented by the family tradition as a whole. If in so doing I include other details of the family chronicle I trust they will not be lacking in interest.

So far as religious influences are in question, it is true that our mother was the daughter of a Presbyterian minister, pastor for many years in Dobbs Ferry, N.Y. Our father, a journalist in New York and then in Madison, Wisconsin, later consul general in Hong Kong and Shanghai, was a devout Congregational layman, concerned for family worship in the home and for Christian education in the Sunday school and in school and college. As a consul he was a friend and supporter of missionaries in China and was later, for a time, in New Haven, the executive secretary of Yale-in-China. This strain of Protestant piety from which most of our oldest colleges in New England arose, and many in the West and South, is also one that has been identified with public concerns and reforming zeal. The life-style of families in this tradition had their disciplines related to worship and the Sabbath and their abstentions from certain social practices associated with "worldliness," but there was no fanaticism or obscurantism as in some forms of Protestant sectarianism.

Cosmopolitan and artistic circles in our cities and intellectuals in our academies are often not well fitted or disposed to understand the so-called Puritan tradition in our culture. It is associated for them with authoritarianism, with special sex attitudes, with the Puritan ethic of work, thrift, and success, with antiaesthetic bias and with law-and-order mentality. The phrase "New England values" sometimes serves as a surrogate. One can pass over any more rigorous tracing of these antecedents. But if we are talking about the American ethos and heritage we should recognize the complexities and the pros and cons of this strain. It is one thing to label its deficiencies and distortions. It is another to come to terms with the stature it has communicated to the human lot and with the moral and creative incentives it has supplied in changing contexts and expressions despite the perversions. It is always so with a great religious tradition, Christian, Jewish, or other.

Many sophisticated circles today stand at such a distance from the kind of home represented by that of our parents that they can only misread the record. This is related to a wider inability to understand important aspects of American culture, and therefore of my brother's work, concerns, and audience.

Though the best of our writers emerging from mid-America, from farm and town, were iconoclastic about the folkways, yet their work often honored the basic vitality and potential. This is true of Faulkner. Visitors have reported that Gertrude Stein could angrily explode when referred to as an "expatriate", and her persistent fascination with the American type in its common denominator is well known, not only in her *The Making of Americans*. The case of Stein is particularly relevant to the work of Wilder since this is one of the areas where their exchange was most vigorous. For this issue one could also cite the case of Glenway Wescott. Coming from the same state as my brother he wrote *Goodbye, Wisconsin,* and went to Paris to seek those old societies where traditions are preserved "of the conduct of life with death in mind."[7] But Wescott could also pay tribute to his pioneer stock in his book, *The Grandmothers*. And he could describe the "midland" as a

> great maternal source of, among other things, ability and brutal ardor and ingenuity and imagination—scarcely revisited, abandoned, almost unable to profit by its fruitfulness in men.[8]

But many representatives of the modern critical movement today and many of our writers are out of touch with these deeper roots in the American reality. If Walt Whitman is honored, it is in terms of his assertion of new-world independence or his new poetic rather than of his democratic vision.

[7]*Goodbye, Wisconsin.* New York, 1928, p. 34.
[8]Ibid., p. 26.

In characterizing the life-style of our home and parents I am concerned to distinguish it from some properly suspect forms of traditional religiosity. There are many differing aspects and amalgams of the Calvinist and wider Protestant heritage in our society, some gone to seed and devitalized, some ingrown and anachronistic, some noxious, some absorbed into the Philistinism of the setting; but some still carriers of the visions and disciplines of the great Reformers, as well as of Milton and Bunyan, of George Fox and the Wesleys, and of many of the early settlers of this country. Granted all due appreciation of the ethnic pluralism and diverse cultural contributions in our population it would be a mistake to underestimate this particular strain and its contemporary permutations, whether political, moral, or cultural.

The term *Puritan* applied to our parents and to the culture in our home is therefore imprecise and misleading. It is also an exaggeration to say, as does one biographer, that my brother came of "a long line of New England divines." On the Wilder side they are hard to find in any direct line. The kind of New England tradition represented on our mother's side is suggested by her grandfather, Arthur Tappan, friend of William Lloyd Garrison and himself the first president of the American Anti-Slavery Society (1837). A philanthropist—like his brother Lewis Tappan who financed the defense of the Spanish slaves in the Amistad slave ship case all the way up to the Supreme Court —he helped fund the establishment of Oberlin College because it was the first to welcome Black as well as women students. He and his New York store were repeatedly in danger from proslavery mobs. This kind of Puritan tradition is no reproach.

The kind of piety represented by the Congregationalism on my father's side was similar, as is suggested by the fact that he chose schools like Oberlin, Mt. Holyoke, and Northfield for his children's education. The books of our father in our possession, which are the most marked up and annotated by him, are Boswell's life of Johnson, the four-volume life of Garrison by his sons and Whittier's poems. Favorites in our family Sunday reading along with the Bible were the works of Bunyan, John Woolman, George Fox, and Thoreau. This kind of Nonconformist tradition is very different from some kinds of

Bible-belt piety and life-style as well as from familiar strains of Calvinist orthodoxy.

The cultural level of the home, suggested by our father's doctorate from Yale and our mother's participation in French and Italian literary circles at Madison and Berkeley, could hardly be viewed as stifling. The situation was not similar to that of other writers who were contemporaries of my brother and who broke sharply with their family patterns of fundamentalist or pietistic character, or to that of a Robinson Jeffers whose father was a biblical scholar in a rigid Calvinist line.

Contemporary intellectuals still have much to learn about the significance and vicissitudes of Calvinism in America from such writers as Perry Miller or the more recent revisionists of Miller, and should be better acquainted with the diverse moral and religious patterns of the midland. They would have a better understanding of the so-called civic religion of the populace and of the contemporary moral or moralistic groundswell as it bears on our politics. But they could also better assess the "political myth" and the social imagination of our society as these reject or react to aesthetic importations from Europe or the Far East. Critics of American religiosity and of home-spun virtues or scruples should also understand that particular patterns of nurture and excellence are always associated with intransigences which can well appear benighted to the emancipated and to those who view them from the outside.

IV

The early Wisconsin years of our family (1894–1906) suggest a number of observations. Although through our parents we had Maine and Hudson River antecedents these were now overlaid with Middle Western experience in depth. It was not just a question of regional but of social variety. A newspaperman like our father was involved in the full gamut of town and country life. Madison, though the state capital and seat of a university, in those days before the motor car was still only a large town. The *Wisconsin State Journal* served the county and the region. My father's editorials for which he is still remembered show his immersion in the folkways and his plebeian sympathies. Well prepared by his doctorate in political science and his years in journalism in New York and elsewhere, he identified himself vigorously with the "Wisconsin progressivism" of the time which was drawing national attention. But it was especially his inimitable "human-interest" editorials which were cherished and copied far and wide. Here sentiment, fancy, eloquence, and humor combined. Those same antennae for the common life and those fine filaments of the poetic and the histrionic which later evoked Grover's Corners in the son had their antecedents in the father. From his college days at Yale as "fence orator" and Glee Club antic he was remembered as word painter, mimic, and clown. In Wisconsin as scribe and as favored speaker at county fair and at Chautauqua he was a poet and wit of the Midland.

In observance of its centennial the *Wisconsin State Journal* included a historical section in its issue of October 5, 1957. Here one can find an account of Amos P. Wilder's years as sub-editor and editor of the paper (1894–1906). A special section is given to the following:

No history of the *Wisconsin State Journal* would be complete without a classic example of the style of Amos P. Wilder when he was editor . . .

The article, "He Gave Her a Lily,"—widely printed and reprinted—is a good example of his brilliant style. The locale was a Ringling-Circus parade in the streets of Madison. A bespangled and painted equestrienne looked down from her horse into the eyes of awe and wonderment of a typical country urchin.

He stretched out his hand and offered her a flower. Leaning over, she accepted his humble offering. Around this incident, Wilder wove an enchanting story which ends:

"Somewhere on the lake shore in Dane County tonight is a boy to whom a hayfield will never seem quite the same. A lady from the marvelous world smiled on him and took his modest gift, and her gentle voice thanked him.

"And somewhere in the confusion of wagon wheels and ghostly mountains of canvas and gilt and gold that look best at a distance

—somewhere in that gay scene of Jerusalem and the Crusades is a woman whose heart quickened today because a barefoot boy was proud to toss her a water lily, and because its fragrance wafted into her dusty, tired life memories of some quiet spot where she dreamed and perhaps loved, and where there was no tread of elephants nor noisy blare of bands, but only green trees and a brook, and the sweet memory of the wind through the trees.''

My father thought there was no experience for a growing boy more valuable than working in a country store or on a farm. He never succeeded in getting us into a store, but the children were placed on a Dane County farm in the earliest years. Later, in the summer of 1915 Thornton was assigned to the farm of the Mt. Hermon School in Northfield, Massachussetts; to a long hot summer with myself on the Dutton farm in Dummerston, Vermont, in 1916; and to the Berea College farm in 1917. All this was part of what our parent called ''broadening experience.'' As further illustration I note that I myself, by his arrangement, put in time in California on a Saratoga farm (prunes and apricots), on a ranch (citrus fruits), and later on an Ohio farm near Oberlin. Our sisters were sent to such wholesome regimes as that at Battle Creek, Michigan or a 4-H camp. During a Christmas holiday special instruction for two of us was set up in the Pomona College observatory since one sister was then in high school in Claremont. When World War I had begun, plans were mooted to involve the older children in volunteer service abroad.

Though the family's financial situation was straitened, the object of all such moves was not first of all self-support on the part of the younger members. The long-range health factor weighed large, but most important was diversity of experience and initiation into varied aspects of the world's work and the common life.

In his educational philosophy my father cherished the neighborly virtues and aspirations of grass-roots America as he had known them in his own Maine childhood. This meant neither Philistinism nor anti-intellectualism. The instincts of the people could be trusted, but they needed committed leaders and spokesmen initiated into their experience, but also equipped with every advantage of education and culture, above all with moral earnestness. At the turn of the century he and his Madison paper, as indicated, were identified with many aspects of Wisconsin progressivism, though he later broke with the senior La Follette when the latter's reform movement appeared to him to have become tarnished with demagoguery. His friends during this period included such pioneers in the social sciences at the University of Wisconsin as F. R. Commons, Richard T. Ely, and E. A. Ross.

His pragmatic outlook was no doubt colored by a certain suspicion whether of bohemia or of academia. One could not get too much education but he was always warning against a sheltered kind of learning which he associated with trifling and parlor games. Standards like Dickens, Scott, and Thackeray were read aloud in the home, besides the spiritual classics I have mentioned for Sundays. But such authors as Byron, Wilde, and Hardy were looked on as "worldly." (It was our mother who took us as children to the Lyric Theater in Oakland to see plays of Ibsen and Shaw. I remember particularly a dramatization of Hardy's *Tess of the D'Urbervilles*.) Earnestness was certainly important, and awareness of a troubled world.

His later Hong Kong journal shows him reflecting on brutalities and suicides among the Western military and social circles on the island, and on the gulf between diplomatic formalism and the teeming humanity of the Far East. It is in this light that one should understand his playful disparagement of Thornton's early literary attempts as "carving cherry stones." If this son and the rest of us gave signs of becoming eggheads he could accept it, but he was at least determined that we should have some basic substratum of shirt-sleeve experience and the kind of sympathies which earned William Jennings Bryan the title of "the Great Commoner."

To suggest the today puzzling outlook of this zealous parent—indirectly evoked in the George Brush of *Heaven's My Destination*—I interject here mention of two of his later editorials, which, as it were, box the compass and illustrate both what would be called narrow-mindedness and its opposite. "The Exposure of a Smarty" refers to a censorship trial of H.L. Mencken in Boston and an article by the latter characterized by the *New York Herald Tribune* as "revolting." My father's editorial speaks of

> this literary mountebank who has too long abused the patience of
> America which is frankly feeling round for a modern literature and is
> pressed by this animated brass monkey to accept his leadership . . . It
> ought to be possible in sane and sensible Massachusetts to clog and
> annoy this pestiferous shark of better men's repute and gadfly of the
> dignities and integrities of life . . . Every country store and every city
> group has some irritable dyspeptic man or woman who has lost the
> vision and enjoys local repute for a sharp tongue and "keen-kutter"
> capacity. Mencken is the high priest of this sort of thing . . .

But another aspect of the senior Wilder's zeal appears in another New
Haven editorial, "The Passing of Latin." This argument for the
retention of the ancient languages in the Yale curriculum was so
eloquent that, on the testimony of a well-placed authority, "it forced
the Yale Corporation to stay its hand before throwing out the
classics."

V

In any case our family's early experience and our father's plebeian
sympathies left their impress on my brother. His precocious aestheticism, his chafing at parental decrees, and his later sophistication did
not alienate him from the poignancies and ordeals of the commonplace, or the deeper root systems of our American way. If this was a
handicap to him as an artist in an age of iconoclasm perhaps time will
vindicate him. Meanwhile his tapping of hidden springs in our folkways appears to have found answering responses in other societies,
notably in Germany.

His fabulation and whatever "affirmation" or celebration may be
reflected in it go deeper than the particular homespun or bourgeois
settings of the novels or plays in question. *Our Town* is not a period
piece or a genre painting but a universal triptych in which our deeper
American pieties rejoin those of a wider humanity. In this horizon all
those questions of social realism or psychological perception, so

essential to much of our best modern literature, are not in question. But neither is there anything here which disallows such concerns.

Perhaps our father's insistence on the exposure of his children to bucolic and shirt-sleeve experience may be looked on as banal or romantic. Perhaps this crusading and pragmatic journalist had too much faith in Peoria. Perhaps this New England mold of conscience and sentiment was ill-adapted to a new age and unattuned to new aesthetic sensibilities. Nevertheless the basic orientation in what was important in our American reality was there and was carried over into my brother's outlook.

One aspect of this indebtedness is reflected in remarks of Thornton cited in Richard Goldstone's *Paris Review* interview with him in 1957.[9] Speaking there of his reasons for interrupting his literary career and volunteering for service in World War II he observes that he sought the benefit of "being thrown into daily contact with non-artists." The acquaintance of young American writers "should include those who have read only *Treasure Island* and have forgotten that." And further, "it would be a very wonderful thing if we see more and more works which close the gulf between the highbrows and the lowbrows."

Of course one can say that there is nothing remarkable about this writer's familiarity with nonacademic strata in our society or his immediate awareness of the life of the many. Many of our artists are born into this kind of background. But it is a question of empathy and perspective. It is a question of recognizing the deeper myth within the moralities and rituals and conformities of Main Street itself. Too many of our intellectuals and writers are captured by the emancipations of the time to the point that they become deracinated. The liberating arts of the epoch have their undeniable importance and stature, not least in their wrestling with our modern disarray. But the imagination forfeits due nourishment when the archetypes are silenced.

This kind of initiation into the grass roots and the buried dreams gestating there is reflected in *The Eighth Day* and in *Heaven's My Destination*, which incidentally imports a reference to Ludington, the

[9]Number 15 (Winter 1957), pp. 37-57.

Michigan conference center where Oberlin students used to wait table in the summer vacations, just as *Our Town* picks up an allusion to North Conway, New Hampshire, where I had a rural pastorate. The *Our Town* locale and characters go back not only to the Peterborough neighborhood of the MacDowell Colony but also to my brother's summers on farms in the same region. Common to all these writings is the empathy for the small town and the struggling families, the tapestry of lives and genealogies, the anonymous multitudes and their livelihoods. But this plebeian vision had already been manifest in "A Happy Journey to Trenton and Camden" and "The Long Christmas Dinner." Even more important, it links up with the sense of what it is to be an American as explored in Thornton's Charles Eliot Norton lectures at Harvard on Emerson, Thoreau, and Dickinson and his Frankfurt address on "Culture in a Democracy," all related to Gertrude Stein's writing on America and his conversations with her.

The point I am making here is that if my brother had not only a democratic outlook but a profound sense of the potential of the many, he was indebted for these to the family tradition, including its religious underpinnings, and to his father's impress and educational dogmas. One can read both the benefits and the liabilities of the paternal role between the lines of his Frankfurt address. This manifesto, spoken in German, took the form of a challenge to the elitism of the European but also the whole Western tradition, and this in the presence of the then President of the West German Republic and other officials, as well as of Albert Schweitzer and Carl J. Burckhardt. Citing Walt Whitman, as already noted, and identifying T. S. Eliot by name as representative of a feudal or elitist outlook, he spoke for "our belief in the potentialities—the so to speak intuitive capabilities—of the average man existing in a democracy," and he called for recognition of "as yet unknown factors, the characteristics of the Man with Head Raised."

The address, which will be found at the close of this essay, raised something of a storm in the German press which continued for some time. *Die Zeit* (then, Hamburg) sent a copy of it to Eliot, together with a critique of it by Rudolf Walter Leonhardt ("Goethe—eine Schmähung der Demokratie?"). Eliot's reply was printed in the Feuilleton of *Die Zeit* (November 14, 1957). He wrote that it was difficult for him to comment on the speech of Mr. Wilder "inasmuch as it seems to me a piece of hysterical nonsense." Further, ". . . this democracy which should have no elite at all and which should fulfill Mr. Wilder's ideals of the common, the ordinary and the vulgar, could only lead to a mass society ruled by a dictatorship or a rigid bureaucratic class . . . Mr. Wilder should also reconsider his theology."

Thornton did not respond to the editor's invitation to reply to Eliot. Many German admirers took his side in the controversy. An able mediating discussion of the issue between Eliot and Wilder was written by Gerhard Hensel,[10] the translator into German of Eliot's *Notes Toward a Definition of Culture*. In his address my brother speaks repeatedly about the perils also for the arts of an egalitarian society or mass culture. But he also says much about the "feudal lie" in accordance with which privilege was passed on from generation to generation "with the chromosomes," and the majority of mankind were deprived not only of social equality but spiritual dignity. Now, however, in the age of the common man, despite the leveling, or rather just because of it, Thornton saw unpredictable creative possibilities, "the peculiar endowments" of a human nature no longer servile.

In a letter Thornton wrote me not long after the episode, he said: "I'd hoped the ripples and eddies of the Frankfurt affair had died down; though I don't regard that as a bad speech. My mistake there was that I did not sufficiently indicate that it was intended to be a bit playful and 'may one say' and 'look at it this way' ("a bit *spielend* and *darf mann sagen* and *schau'n-Sie-mal*")."

In the address the speaker sought to demonstrate the persistence of feudal categories of elitism and privilege in common language usage. He noted the demeaning associations (in both German and English) of such terms as *common* and *vulgar*. More particularly he pointed to the status implications hidden in such adjectives as *noble (edel)*, *lordly (herrlich)*, and *gentle* (as in *gentleman*). But in all such pervasive categories the *ignoble* and the *lowborn* (contrast such titles

---

[10] *Die Zeit*, July 11, 1958.

as *Hoch wohlgeborenen*), the *common* and the *ordinary*, are robbed not only of their social but of their spiritual worth. The speaker also showed the connection of such distinctions of superiority-inferiority to the age-old status of woman in our tradition.

My brother also urged that all such prejudicial distinctions had long been fortified by the authoritarian connotations of the term *father* both in the family and in religion. The address elicited protests from the religious press in Germany because of its claim that "God is not Father, but Spirit." But Thornton's concern was with the hierarchical implications for society when patriarchal views of God as King and Father lend sanction to human orders of subordination. It is in this light that he continues:

> One of the principal evils of this confusion was the image of the son.
>
> No man has a father after twenty-one. Lucky is the man who, after twenty-one, has in his father his best friend.
>
> A son until twenty-one is obedient: thereafter—not.

This passage no doubt reflects my brother's own dilemma with an overshadowing parent. But for the main democratic theme of the address as a whole he is no less surely indebted to the same parent. There is nothing about this kind of ambivalence that should surprise us.

There is a moving detail in a recently published tribute by Cyril Connolly to W. H. Auden. The former cites Auden's line, "From the immense bat-shadow of home deliver us." Acting on a prompting by Auden in line with this independence, Connolly tells us how he impatiently wounded his father, brought tears to his eyes, and later regretted it. Auden's advice to his friend in this instance had been too ruthless.[11]

In the *Paris Review* interview mentioned above the questioner asked Wilder at one point: " . . . do you feel that you were born in a place and at a time, and to a family—all of which combined favorably

[11] In *W. H. Auden: A Tribute*, Stephen Spender, ed. New York, 1975, p. 71.

to shape you for what you were to do?'' His reply was in part:

> By the standards of many people, and by my own, these dispositions
> were favorable;—but what are our judgments in such matters?
> Everyone is born with an array of handicaps—even Mozart, even
> Sophocles—and acquires new ones . . . . The most valuable thing I
> inherited was a temperament that does not revolt against Necessity and
> that is constantly renewed in Hope (I am alluding to Goethe's great
> poem about the problem of each man's ''lot''—the *Orphische
> Worte).* [12]

In a letter to myself of about 1968, apropos of the prospect of an
operation, Thornton cited the fourth stanza of Goethe's poem,
''Urworte: Orphisch,'' entitled ''Nötigung'' (Necessity).

> Da ists dann wieder, wie die Sterne wollten:
> Bedingung und Gesetz; und aller Wille
> Ist nur ein Wollen, weil wir eben sollten,
> Und vor dem Willen schweigt die Willkür stille;
> Das Liebste wird vom Herzen weggescholten,
> Dem harten Muss bequemt sich Will und Grille.
> So sind wir scheinfrei denn, nach manchen Jahren
> Nur enger dran, als wir am Anfang waren. [13]

He added: ''That's not Stoic—but as his 'Orphisch' suggests—
pre-Socratic mysticism. You adapt yourself to necessity—*nach
manchen Jahren*—as though it were a choice.''

---

[12]P. 43.

[13]So is it then again as the stars would have it:
Limit and Law − and, since we are behoven,
''I will'' yields to ''I would''
And chance desires are stilled before that willing;
That which is dearest is harried from the heart,
Will and caprice bow to the austere ''Must.''
So we are seeming-free, after many a year,
Nearer at least thereto than in the beginning.

My brother cherished this motif and this particular expression of it. He also recognized it in Hölderlin. One of the reasons he was so appreciated in German student circles was that he knew their poetry and drama intimately and could discuss it with them, in German, in this searching way. He would address them as "meine Kinder," and both scold them and be playful with them. They valued the plays of O'Neill, Tennessee Williams, and Arthur Miller, but this was another kind of American contact. They called him their "Amerikanischer Onkel."

In this connection I interject here another reminiscence about Thornton's partiality for Goethe and his acquaintance with German language and literature. Though his earliest models for prose style were such English and French writers as Cardinal Newman and Mme. de Sévigné his study of German at Oberlin College remained important to him. This initiation there was shared with his friend Robert M. Hutchins. They carried this common enthusiasm into later life, as is specially evident in Hutchins' inviting Thornton to speak at the Goethe Festival at Aspen in 1949. At that assembly Wilder assisted at the podium in the translation of Albert Schweitzer's Germany address,[14] as he did on another day for Ortega y Gasset's Spanish lecture.[15] In those years when Thornton was teaching for Hutchins at the University of Chicago a pleasant tradition reports the following. When they encountered each other crossing the quadrangles they had a little game with each other. One would immediately cite a quotation from Goethe and the other would respond instanter with another. This exchange of a Goethe password evidently went back to their Oberlin days and to their student associations at Yale.

---

[14]A piquant coincidence emerged in this connection. Schweitzer remarked to Thornton that another Wilder had served him as amanuensis at Oxford in 1922 in connection with his Dale lectures there in French on Ethics and Civilization. The lectures were given at Mansfield College where I was a student. My services to him were confined to assisting him with his correspondence for a week or so, and showing him the way to the two organs for his Bach concerts at Christ Church and New College. When Schweitzer learned that we were brothers he wrote me a gracious note from Aspen.

[15]The more precise circumstances of these translations appear in a letter of

But to return to the Goethe motif of Necessity or *Ananke*. Thornton could recur to the theme in connection with the famous words inscribed by Beethoven at the close of his last string quartet: "Muss es sein? Es muss sein!" As Leslie Parnas, the distinguished cellist, has remarked, this affirmation of Necessity is not a matter of resignation. For the meaning one must turn to the music itself, especially to the incomparable slow movement. Its inviolate serenity exhibits the transcendence and invention opened up by free consent to the inexorable. Thornton was fond of colloquializing this idea of accepting Fate or what cannot be altered. Over against those who chafe at existence and whose days are lacerated with resentments he set the equipoise of the beleaguered man or woman who says of his or her trapped condition, "I like," or "I like what I got." (It would be a crass confusion of categories to identify such acceptance with social or political irresponsibility.)

This digression has not been irrelevant to my reminiscences of the family. I have cited Thornton's statement that he was indebted for this outlook to his inheritance.

VI

In speaking of the early Wisconsin years of the family I have been led to anticipate somewhat on the themes of my brother's grass-roots initiation and the paternal role. Some further account of our father's career may be of interest and will fill out the picture of the inheritance in question.

As I have indicated, our father's Madison paper first supported La Follette's progressive crusades and his campaign against the railroad power in the state and only later (1904) sided with the Republican

---

Thornton's to me from Aspen at the time. "I've become the packmule of the convocation. Dr. Schweitzer gave his lecture in French last night. Translation made in New York by some journalistic hack or by one of those *ancillae* that smother Mahatmas. Terrible. The English text was read antiphonally with Dr. S. from the platform.—Today I was sent for. Would I touch up the English text for its German presentation tomorrow and would I read it antiphonally for him?—Ditto: Don José Ortega y Gasset. Only for him I am to be first and only translator of his Second Lecture and I am to read it with him from the Podium."

"stalwarts" against him. Meanwhile he became widely known through his addresses in the East and articles in various journals as an interpreter of Wisconsin progressivism. Under William Graham Sumner at Yale he had written the first doctoral dissertation on municipal government in any of our universities. At Madison his coaching of talented young reporters and his editorials became quasi-legendary. Many stories were told of his unconventional assignments and irascible fiats in the editor's sanctum, and he took pride in the fact that his was the first daily paper which refused to accept liquor advertisements. A later chronicler reports that "he started several of the city's most important cultural and civic movements."

All this led to the distinction of his appointment as consul general in Hong Kong, one of the top consular positions at that time, and one requiring confirmation by the U.S. Senate. After six months our mother brought the four children back to this country for better schooling than could then be had in Hong Kong, and we all attended the public schools in Berkeley. This was in 1906 when Thornton was nine years of age.

These years of separation—lasting until 1911 when my father had been moved to Shanghai—were sometimes desperately difficult for our mother, who had four young children to care for with very limited funds. They had nevertheless their redeeming features. In Berkeley as earlier in Madison our mother had friends in the university faculty. She was active in both French and Italian circles, and we have her own translations of poems by Verhaeren and Carducci in her collections of these poets. At one time her earlier Sunday school teacher in Dobbs Ferry, New York, William Lyon Phelps, was teaching in the English department, and the Ernest Hockings were at the university. We children took part in the mob scenes in the plays put on in the Greek Theater by the classics department. We likewise took part in the Nativity tableaux in our church, and my brother's work early and late prolongs such initiations.

Thornton's literary precocity, taste, and range should certainly be traced to our mother's influence and encouragement from these early years. Our musical initiation went back to the Wisconsin period and to her love of the piano. In that time also, with Madison friends, she had frequently attended the opera in Chicago, and had visited the museums of Europe. It was through her literary acquaintance and associations that Thornton became aware of European writers and dramatists. As he himself began to write in his school days she was always his confidante and stimulus. How far this went is particularly clear later in his letters to her from Rome, Florence, and Paris in 1920–1921. Here he tells her of his first encounter with the theater of Pirandello, of his reading, and of his own narrative and dramatic projects and revisions—all assured of an instructed and delighted response.

One special feature of the Berkeley period is worth recalling. My father sent over now one and then another Chinese youth to further their education and to assist in the home. One came from a Cantonese coolie family. Another was later picked out by him from an orphanage in Shanghai and served him for a time as office boy. When they arrived in California they spoke only pidgin English. Though they were fifteen or sixteen years old they were enrolled in the earliest primary grades. Children of both of these later took doctorates at the University of California.

Their lifelong devotion to our family and to my father—on the pattern of Chinese filial loyalty—was remarkable and moving. In one case the oldest son was named for our father (Amos Wilder Yong), and this has been carried over to a second generation. In the other case, some years after the death of our parents, the former servant, though he could ill afford it, came East by bus from California to carry out what he felt was an obligation to my father to show continuing solicitude for us, the children, and especially our sisters. One can appreciate from such examples why old China hands have such a marveling faith in the fiber and capacities of the Chinese common people.

In Hong Kong, of course, my father was accredited to the British governor of the island but his diplomatic and mercantile functions extended to Canton and the mainland. In Shanghai the extraterritorial situation of the Western powers brought with it judicial duties as well. Since this city was the focus of the Chinese revolution in 1911 the senior Wilder was well acquainted with the revolutionary leaders. He also traveled widely in China and in contrast with many such officials was a friend and counselor of American missionaries, especially in their roles in medicine, education, and famine relief.

Thornton's own residence in China was confined to the six months in Hong Kong and to one year when he attended the China Inland Mission School in Chefoo after the family was reunited in Shanghai. It is surely far-fetched to assign a strain of Oriental mysticism in his later work to this experience, as one handbook does. But recurrent emphasis in his writings on the myriads of human beings who have lived and died, that telescopic view of humanity instanced in the words of the Stage Manager in *Our Town* about all that was going on in ancient Babylon—this vision Thornton himself traced to his China experience.

In his Shanghai post my father initiated the first luncheon club in which Chinese members participated with Western officials and business representatives. A letter from a senior member of the American colony to the *New Haven Journal Courier*, on the occasion of this parent's death in 1936, goes into detail about his contributions to the civic and cultural life of the city and his friendship with the Chinese. This reporter adds that many anticipated that he would have been appointed as our Minister to Peking if his illness had not intervened.[16] Because of his assistance the Wisconsin sociologist, Edward A. Ross, dedicated to him his volume, *The Changing Chinese*,[17] with the following characterization: "Friend of the Changing Chinese, and Eloquent Interpreter to Them of the Best Americanism."

One sidelight on my father's principles is afforded by his refusal as consul general in Hong Kong to cooperate with the project of an American brewer to extend his market to South China. As a matter of fact, this issue arose more than once, also with regard to hard liquor. Wilder should have resigned if he was not willing to accede to the requests of the State Department to assist a legitimate business interest! As a matter of fact, he did offer to resign more than once over

[16]W. W. Lockwood, in the *New Haven Journal Courier*, August 18, 1936.
[17]New York, 1911.

this question but the Department did not press it. In one instance President Taft became involved and the family preserved a letter of his to "Dear Amos," recalling Yale associations (in a Senior Society) and assuring my father that any question of his resignation was excluded. Thornton wrote me once that he had assembled the whole docket of this correspondence to show to Alexander Woollcott and that the latter had registered "immense delight." Thornton continues:

> It's not hard to imagine Taft's enormous bulk shaking with laughter as he remembers "Amos" of the Skull and Bones days going through an agony of spirit on the matter, and answering with affectionate indulgence.

The *Saturday Evening Post* had a photograph of this period showing my father receiving Taft at the Hong Kong waterside from the tender of a U. S. battleship, both with silk hats and frock coats. At this time Taft was Secretary of War. A reinforced sedan chair had been ordered for the guest. The bill of the Chinese merchant read: "Special sedan chair for great American giant."

Consul Wilder's position on the liquor issue was that enough harm had been done in the past by Western complicity in the opium traffic. At any rate more than one view is possible of this kind of attachment to principle. Recent revelations suggest that more of this kind of conscience and backbone, however scrupulous, would not come amiss in our foreign service. Even in the matter of temperance I could cite cases where consular officials were called home, not because they were abstainers but because they were alcoholics.

On one occasion in Shanghai my father welcomed a new consul for a post further inland, and wired ahead to a local American missionary to see that he was properly greeted and introduced to his new office and responsibilities. A few days later this missionary wired back that the new incumbent was drunk and had been playfully firing off his gun at pigeons and Chinese kites from the balcony of the consulate. My father saw to his repatriation. Eight months later his successor was similarly sent on and installed. This time Wilder received the laconic and reassuring wire: "Sober American consul safely arrived."

To any who would see my father's abstemiousness as a grave parental defect I can add further detail. When he was in Shanghai he served only grape juice at the ceremonial outdoor reception on the Fourth of July to the diplomatic corps and other guests. One can appreciate that in a coast port in the Far East this deprivation created a scandal. Old China hands have told us that this austerity evoked consternation and derision, but that after hearing Wilder speak at a few public functions all was forgiven. In view of his wit, mimicry, and eloquence he was often compared at home with the celebrated after-dinner speaker, Chauncey Depew. It is reported that when the next Independence Day reception came around, as a joke on him, some of his friends sent their servants out ahead of time to plant liquor in the shrubbery.

For any who would attempt a Freudian analysis of my brother's development, I call attention to these and other complicated aspects of our father's makeup. In one portrayal this parent is represented as an insensitive autocrat, solely the disciplinarian, even at a distance maintaining a kind of inquisition over and intimidation of his children, politically ambitious himself and intolerant of any frivolity in his offspring such as would be associated with aesthetic or less than robust interests. Especially as regards Thornton this meant unwise fiats as to his schools, and psychological harm.

There is one general remark to be made here. Censorious testimonies as to our father should be placed in context. In our family as in many, one-sided, momentary, and humorous disparagements of a parent can be made, but these should not be pressed into caricature. Our family, for example, has preserved amusing anecdotes as to our father's worries about Thornton's bread-winning prospects. Our Aunt Helen, his sister, once scoffed at him and said that this son would one day be supporting the whole family. The story is that he turned on his heel and left her without a word. Aunt Helen, incidentally, had more confidence in her own problem child, our cousin, the inimitable Wilder Hobson (Yale 1928), who later wrote the first serious study of American jazz[18] and who had a versatile and distinguished career with *Fortune* and *Newsweek*. Hobson's friends in the Century Club in New York or in Squirrel Island, Maine, like Jack Jessup and Glenway Wescott, knew that his quicksilver streak of the histrionic was of the same vintage as that of Thornton, an ebullient vein in the family which they had long recognized in my father.

All this is not to deny that the latter was doctrinaire and heavy-handed in many ways, especially after the loss of health that led to his retirement from the consular service. But experience of life should teach the biographer that these matters of intimate family life are exceedingly complex, and that thwarting factors in the growth of children often elicit compensating energies. Sometimes also, as in our case, the deeper parental securities and orientation communicate themselves in ways that elude particular constraints. My brother could on occasion be sharp about his father and characterize him as "octopus" or a "grudging Isaac" (to his Jacob son). The critic in question draws out a whole scenario about this relationship and in a surprising way speaks of mutual "contempt" and even reads a motif of parricide into the novels and plays.

But this kind of psychologizing is much overplayed. Those who knew the parent can recognize his affectionate and solicitous demeanor to a T in the unremitting zeal of Mr. Antrobus in *The Skin of Our Teeth,* in his coaching of Henry and Gladys in the alphabet and the multiplication table. The paternal image in the play as a whole is far from one of possessiveness or intimidation.

Indeed it is to this paternal relation that a passage like that at the climax of *Our Town* testifies when, on Emily's revisited twelfth birthday, she hears her father call out, "Where's my girl? Where's my birthday girl?" Emily cannot sustain the confrontation. Like Robert Penn Warren at the death of his father,

> I could not move,
> Naked in that black blast of his love.[19]

[18] *American Jazz Music*. New York, 1939.
[19] "Mortmain I," in *You, Emperors and Others: Poems 1957-1960*. New York, 1960, p. 25.

This is as good a point as any at which to comment on my brother's lifelong bachelor state or, as I would say, calling. This can be and has been misconstrued by those who did not know him. More particularly it was open to misconstruction in quarters ruled by current clichés or in which the celibate vocation—whether in religion, science or art—is looked on as incredible or unnatural. Those who knew Thornton in his college years could recognize well enough that he was no less susceptible to romantic responses than his classmates. If more definitive involvements were precluded in his early twenties when he was finding himself, the factors were economic and personal. Thereafter it became a matter of fundamental decision. From college days on his absorption in letters and in the fertility of his imagination, in opening powers and projects, became so imperative that he was caught up in this commitment. It was not only a question of domesticity. Even earlier he had demurred at continuing his college course.

One can find an analogy of this kind of austere and supervening dedication—to be sure with different involvements—in the correspondence of Coleridge and Wordsworth at the outset of their shared excitements, reflected in *The Prelude* in which the latter speaks of vows both imposed and accepted. In any case with Thornton the special calling crystallized apart from marriage. At some point it took the form of a grave and irreversible choice, not without awareness of its human costs, and not unrelated to the theme of Necessity or *Ananke* to which I have referred, but seen by him as that kind of paradoxical constraint which empowers.

Here I conclude this selective and what may seem gratuitous review of family matters. My aim has been in part to correct whatever misleading impressions may be current as to my brother's early influences and development, but mainly to call attention to widely underestimated legacies in the American spectrum, which indeed are but prolongations of older and more universal pieties.

It is, as I have said, a very shallow judgment to look on *Our Town* as only a period piece or New England daguerrotype in the line, say, of Sarah Orne Jewett.

If the task of many modern masters has been both to "make it new" and to forge the conscience and sensibility of a new epoch, this has not annulled another calling of the fabulist, one for which Dante acknowledged his indebtedness to Brunetto Latini:

M'insegnavate come l'uom s'eterna.[20]

In this respect one can see how fitting it is that the scene of the last act of *Our Town*—the village dead sitting on their graves—should have modeled itself in part on the last engraving of William Blake's Everyman series, "The Gates of Paradise."

VII

This brings us back to the basic issue as to the task and options of modern letters. I have suggested at a number of points that the whole program of modern revolt and iconoclasm has bypassed certain abiding aspects of our deeper human reality. This liberating movement, moreover, may have reached its term. No doubt in our intellectual life and in our arts there is always a demand for critical and imaginative exploration. But the particular antibourgeois, anti-Victorian, and antinomian reaction now in our time shows diminishing returns. In Trilling's terms the "adversary" aspect of liberal culture and the liberal imagination becomes itself open to question. Once this situation is recognized, there may well be a radical reassessment of the period we have passed through, and of its writers and artists, its critical schools and their premises.

As a suggestion of how the work of Thornton Wilder fits into such a picture I call attention to a recent statement by a German critic. In January 1976, following Wilder's death, a commemorative observance was held in the Civic Theater of Freiburg, participated in by theatrical groups of the city and the English-American Seminar of the University of Freiburg. Two of his one-act plays were produced. An address, "Hommage à Thornton Wilder," was given by Professor

---

[20] "You taught me how man makes himself eternal," *Inferno*, xv, 85.

Franz H. Link, a scholar who has written extensively on American literature.[21]

In his tribute the speaker first develops a somewhat detailed parallel between the careers and stagecraft of Wilder and Bertolt Brecht. Born within a year of each other, they each achieved a worldwide public, Wilder with *The Bridge of San Luis Rey* in 1927 and Brecht with his *Dreigroschenoper* in 1928. After a period of silence during the Nazi period and World War II "they dominated the literary scene in decisive fashion."

> While Brecht coined the conceptions of "epic theater" and of "Verfremdung" . . . Wilder developed contemporaneously and independently his conception of the incorporation of the audience in the action by abolishing the Fourth Wall of proscenium drama and bringing to consciousness "the value of the least important events of daily life." What Brecht much later characterized as "Verfremdung" Wilder had exploited in the Three Minute Plays which he was already writing as an undergraduate. In his "Pullman Car Hiawatha" and in "A Happy Journey to Trenton and Camden" he introduced the Stage Manager, and in *Our Town* assigned him a major role, thus greatly influencing the modern theatre. With "The Long Christmas Dinner" and *The Skin of Our Teeth* he broke with all existing conventions of temporal sequence. Through time-montage, anachronism and actor-play he merged the time staged with that of the beholder. Brecht wrote plays-to-instruct ("Lehrstücke"). Wilder also thought of himself with undisguised irony as "schoolmaster."

Link then notes that in our later time Brecht is looked on as the great renewer of the modern theater, while Wilder is characterized as "classicist" and "humanist"—"with the clear implication: not wholly at home in our time." Why so?

> One can answer such questions easily by observing that two elements are almost missing in Wilder, elements which pass today as modern, but which should rather in view of their overemphasis be identified as fashionable. These are, on the one hand, social indictment, and, on

---

[21] Published as "Das Amerikanische und das Menschliche bei Thornton Wilder," *Der Rotarier,* Hamburg, Jahrgang 26, Heft 307 (June 1976), 383-387.

the other, the abolishing of taboos in the sexual domain – manifestations of our often misconceived legacies from Marx and Freud. But is our time which so willingly identifies itself as pluralistic to be defined by this inheritance alone? That this need not be the case is witnessed by the work of Thornton Wilder; and certainly not because he falls back on positions which were rendered obsolete by the two elements in question; but because he occupies a position in his time which it is essential to grasp as an alternative.

It may well be illuminating for our own American assessment of Wilder's contribution to see how he is judged in this European perspective. In his own way, and in a larger context, Link confirms my own thesis that the tasks and options of modern letters are more diverse than is commonly recognized by the critical consensus of the period.

Link returns to this issue in connection with my brother's controversial address at Frankfurt in 1957. This frontal attack on elitism disturbed his conservative following among German readers and playgoers. But the theme of the common man as hero also alienated the radicals there whose hero was not the common man but the revolutionary. Thus Wilder's hero, anonymous and self-denying, Mr. Antrobus or George Brush or Alcestis or John Ashley—the hero as fool or incognito—could appear as either offensively egalitarian or uncommitted in Germany or he could appear as banal or sentimental in America. But in *Our Town* and in *The Eighth Day,* if the author is glorifying the commonplace and the diurnal, it is not a question of their actuality but of their promise. It is a question of the hidden figure in the tapestry and of that remnant which, if it be an elite, is one that does not so recognize itself, but which "transmits fairer messages than it is itself aware of."

But this dimension is one widely forgotten in the main preoccupations of our period and its letters. It is not as though my brother lacked initiation into our modern climate and the terms it has set for art and communication. There is no conflict between his vision or his scenarios and the main thrust of liberation in our age. They may, however, speak for universal impulses otherwise neglected or smothered—

which would account for the continuing appeal of his work to so many differing publics.

Well-grounded and comprehensive criticism of the work of Thornton Wilder in this country has still to be awaited. Until now we have had ad hoc reviews of his works, colorful personalia, and such tentative assessments as are to be found in the familiar manuals. As Malcolm Cowley has recently remarked: "... those ateliers (i.e., of the Upper West Side or Greenwich Village) have failed to discuss his work, and so, unfortunately, have most of our serious critics. In point of intelligent criticism, Wilder is the most neglected author of a brilliant generation."[22] Even the appreciations of such commentators as Edmund Wilson, Glenway Wescott, and Edmund Fuller relate only to controversial issues or to limited aspects of his work. American critics should be aware of the more serious analyses of the plays and novels that have been carried out abroad. Such matters as his dramaturgy, his Americanism, his use of classical sources, the variety of his genres, and the ways in which any thematic is absorbed and hidden in his art—all such features are pursued in a wide compass of comparative literary survey.

Where critics dominated by the Zeitgeist and its aesthetic canons charge the author of *Our Town* and *The Eighth Day* with a superficial didactic moralism or optimism, the Swiss critic Emil Staiger can point to more fundamental categories. In his tribute to my brother at the recent ceremony in Bonn of the Order, "Pour le Mérite," this master in the field of German literature spoke of the hopefulness in his outlook in the following terms, with special reference to *The Eighth Day:*

> What he has in mind is not the kind of Philistine hope which deceives itself with words but *elpis thraseia,* that bold venture of the human spirit unintimidated by *Ananke,* the beating of whose wings, as Goethe says, leaves aeons behind it.[23]

---

[22] *New York Times Book Review,* December 21, 1975.

[23] The eulogy was delivered June 2, 1976 in the Aula of the University of Bonn. It was printed in *Das Parlament,* Bonn, no. 31 (July 31, 1976), p. 10, and in the publications of the Order, "Reden und Gedenkworte," Heidelberg, 1976/77. The Goethe reference is to the fifth stanza of "Urworte: Orphisch."

The modern sensibility has long been in an understandable reaction against what it calls Victorian optimism and any kind of affirmation that may appear linked with privilege or an outworn idealism, religious or secular. But there are three remarks to make here. In the first place, the real issue is not between affirmation and negation, but between authenticity and sentimentalism. Optimism and pessimism are both sentimental and neither one should interest us. Just as there are modern moods of masochism and iconoclasm which are self-indulgent, so there are levels of celebration which are properly disabused and free of all romanticism.

Second, where the literary arts are in question, the real issue with respect to world view and philosophy of life is not one of didactics but of the imagination. The test is in the fabulation, the poiesis, and the dramaturgy. Whether Wilder's "hopefulness" or *pietas* is admissible stands or falls with the aesthetic structure of his writings and their resonance in the echoing chambers of the human heart and will. In this area persuasion is not a matter of indoctrination or moralities but of vision.

Thirdly, the real issue is not between moralism and emancipation, whether in life or in art: both involve programs and coercion and neither one should interest us. But the domain of the moralities in the widest sense is another matter, and one inseparable from the humanities generally. The most emancipated critic can hardly fail to recognize that the supreme classics of our tradition have had to do with moralities and in a normative sense. In our age for special reasons the term *moralities* has become ambiguous and has a bad name; the modern artist has to deal with this domain without the name. But the arena and the human agenda remain the same. The real issue is not that of moralism but of stature and humanity.

Many artists today in their concern for the real are content to dismantle the older humanities. This also may be a valid form of wrestling with the stuff of life but it is too often animated by revolt alone. It may also proceed from mistaken premises and straitened imagination. As Emil Staiger observed in his address: "The Western world has gotten used to thinking of despair and *Angst* as deeper than faith and hope." He then cites Wilder: "There is no creativity without faith and hope." "For many," he continues, "that sounds like insipid religiously-colored optimism which flatly contradicts our experience." But he then goes on to show in particulars in the scenarios of my brother's works how hard won is any affirmation.

In short, those alleged moralistic or "Pollyanna" features that are charged against his writings are grounds of offense just because they proceed from both a more austere and a more magnanimous vision of our condition than is current among our intellectuals today. It is also a question of human sympathies and charities which are far removed from the canonical "compassion", "pathos", and "irony" which are the hallmarks of most contemporary fiction and drama. If this combination of severity and mansuetude traces to a Puritan religious perspective on mortal affairs, let the objectors make the most of it. In any case the legacy is mediated in the art, and there are hosts of men and women who are so constituted as to respond.

For the vicissitudes of Thornton Wilder's work and standing among his American critics one can employ the analogy of a card game.

After his first three novels whose settings were in Rome, Peru, and the island of Andros, the critics called for a locale here in the American scene.

Wilder threw down an American card, indeed, a Main Street card, *Heaven's My Destination*, a kind of American *Don Quixote*. The replique is well reflected in a letter mentioning the novel, written by Edmund Wilson at the time to John Dos Passos.

> Thornton Wilder has taken up the challenge flung down by Mike Gold and written the best book of his life. I wish you would overcome your prejudice against him and read it.[24]

But this was not what the players were looking for. They did not know these aspects of Gopher Prairie or Plains, Georgia, very well, and could not identify with this combination of farce and anguish in the grass roots.

[24] Edmund Wilson, *Letters on Literature and Politics, 1912-1972*, Elena Wilson, ed. New York, 1977, p. 256.

For example, R. P. Blackmur reviewed the novel in *The Nation* in June 1935 under the caption, "A Psychogenic Goodness." He argued there that this fable of Christian goodness passing through its awkward age failed to recognize that Christianity was no longer "a fundamental governing assumption in our days." The picaresque hero, George Brush—in contrast for example with Dostoevsky's Alyosha—has not the exceptional force to overcome this handicap. The protagonist and the episodes, therefore, fail to win fictional consent. The dramatic substance seems at a critical point without the authority of art and merely "psychogenic," a matter of intention.

But Blackmur's sense of the context is too rigid. His world is that of the aesthetic modernists and not the actual theater of our American reality. Wilder's novel operates effectively here just because its tragicomic method undermines both belief and disbelief at a level where consent is still open and the answering imagination can be quickened. In a review of Blackmur's best-known work, *The Double Agent,* also in *The Nation* this same year, William Troy, while praising him for the "new-criticism" focus in his approach yet faults him for his failure to relate his findings to "the whole of our intellectual arrangement of experience" and to "the world which surrounds it."

In any case the American novel that Wilder offered to his critics did not meet their tests. Their America was cosmopolite, alienated, and rootless. They kept pressing for an American fiction in these terms.

In the sequel Wilder responded with images of a deeper and more enduring America; as it were outflanking their moves and trumping their expectations: the America of Grover's Corners (*Our Town*); of Excelsior, New Jersey (*The Skin of Our Teeth*); and of Coaltown, Illinois (*The Eighth Day*).

The dealers and arbiters of the game did not recognize these visages of America and could not honor these face cards. In such portrayals they missed the kind of actuality and the range of sophisticated strategies which answered to their own repertoire and with which their hands were well stocked. But the game as they played it had its built-in limitations. Their fables of liberation lacked the deeper octaves and registers. It followed that the naïveté and moral resonances of Wilder's America disoriented them, and they could only see his scenarios as belated or banal.

It is true that beginning in the thirties new aspects of the American scene claimed their attention. In his book, *Native Ground* (1942), Alfred Kazin notes a return to the roots in a chapter entitled "America! America!," having in mind the new regionalism and such work as that of James Agee. But even such moving documentation stopped short of any invocation and celebration of the hidden potential, the obscure transactions, and the plebeian epos of the New World.

What was distinctive in my brother's work was the combination of local and universal in his vision and genres. Intending high praise a German critic observed that certain of his dramas remind us of "ancient morality plays"; and another saw "a return to the world theater of the Middle Ages and the baroque period." To see *Our Town* and *The Skin of Our Teeth* in this light is one way of identifying in them those diapasons and overtones which account for their popular and human appeal. On the other hand it is this nonrealistic optic, this telescopic view, this focus on Everyman or on the Knight of Faith (*The Eighth Day*) which opens them to the charge of allegory or didacticism.

But there are saving features: for one thing, the exceptional variety of the writings whether in method or basic fable. After his earliest work each novel or play represented a radically new departure. This kind of resource in invention and strategy is not consonant with any supposed monolithic intention or message. Masterful improvisation and poiesis took precedence over whatever various motifs or legacies might be drawn into the whole.

Thus, so far as the writings are concerned with moralities the latter are in one way or another absorbed in the fiction or embedded in the art. Where they extrude as in the asides to the audience in *The Skin of Our Teeth* or *The Matchmaker* they are carried by sheer gaiety. More important, however, is the basic question of form and style. Any persuasive artistic presentation of great matters in our day is linked with the modern revolution in genres and method.

Thus, in what concerns stagecraft the universality of *Our Town* is inseparable from its new dramaturgy. Again, it is the German discussion of *The Skin of Our Teeth* which has pointed up the related breakthrough in "epic theater" of Brecht and Wilder. If Brecht's political moralities are carried aesthetically by the stagecraft he employs, so the more general human values of Wilder or Claudel by their respective versions of world theater.

My references here and earlier to special appreciation of my brother's work in Germany require further comment. Especially as shared in by both critics and the wider public this esteem has been a matter of some irritation to certain critical circles in this country. It is true that extraneous factors sometimes operate in Continental assessment of American writers. In point are such cases as those of Bret Harte and Upton Sinclair. More instructive for us has been the resonance abroad of Poe, Walt Whitman, and such a thinker as William James.

In *The Nation* in 1958 the American critic, Paul Fussell, Jr., published a short article entitled, "Thornton Wilder and the German Psyche." As a Fulbright Lecturer in Germany (1957–1958), Fussell had been nonplussed at the popularity of Wilder among his students and in the public. Among intellectuals, it is true, he found that "German taste was generally that of a literate American," oriented to a canon "whose central nervous system was in the line James—Hemingway—Faulkner." But the preferences of the wider public were "for American fictions of the optimistic-coy school, including the work of Saroyan, the later works of Steinbeck, and preeminently all the writings and all the public utterances of Thornton Wilder." Wilder was "hysterically popular in Germany since the end of the war when the State Department sent *Our Town* on tour." Reference is made to the Peace Prize in 1957, to "enlarged displays of Wilder's saintly features," and to his speaking engagements at German universities, in which he dealt with "Large Issues: Love, especially, and Democracy and the virtues of the Common Man." Here, gratifying the European image of what should be, was the American writer, with all the folksy innocence

of evil, and with touching devotion to Love, and with his inspiring
and efficient optimism.

Before proceeding with Fussell's observations it is appropriate
here to cite a witness to Thornton's reception in Germany in the Fall
of 1948. As a background it should be recalled that Robert Hutchins
had just set up an exchange of professors between the University of
Chicago and the University of Frankfurt as a step toward opening up
intellectual and academic relations between Germany and America
after the war. This was all the more desirable since the educational
program of the American Military Government in our zone at that
time was highly rigid, having been conceived in terms of reeducating
Germany along the lines of our own progressive pedagogy. At the
ceremony inaugurating the exchange in the Paulskirche in Frankfurt,
Hutchins, speaking in German, urged that educational policy for the
German schools and universities should be set by their own faculties,
so many of whom had suffered under the Nazi regime. This statement
elicited immense applause which was joined in by the American
educationalists from the Military Government since they did not
know German.

Professor Wilhelm Pauck, then of the University of Chicago and
now at Stanford University, writes as follows about Thornton's
participation in the new venture, at Frankfurt in the Fall of 1948.

> The Chicago-Frankfurt exchange had just begun and we Chicagoans
> stayed in a large villa which had been requisitioned by the American
> Military Government. There were seven or eight of us and Thornton
> was the ninth. Thornton brought much life and excitement into our
> common life. All over Germany the theaters staged *The Skin of Our
> Teeth* and the play was getting a tremendous response. Every morn-
> ing huge packages of mail addressed to Thornton Wilder arrived. A
> special secretary had to be engaged in order to make it possible for
> Thornton to answer at least a few of the letters that were being sent
> to him.
>
> One afternoon he delivered a lecture at the university on the renewal of
> the theater. He spoke in German and his lecture was like an overflow-
> ing fountain. He rapidly spoke a few sentences, then he paused for a
> few minutes, which seemed like an eternity, in order to find the fitting

German word, and then, at the end, one had the impression that Aristotle was dead as the guide to playwrights and that a new day had dawned for the drama.

The Frankfurt theater arranged for an evening with Thornton Wilder and parts of his plays were staged. We Chicagoans were assigned special seats in the orchestra and Thornton sat among us . . .The highlight of the evening was a presentation of the first or last act of *Our Town*, I forget which. But Thornton had agreed to play the part of the Narrator and he spoke his very charming Oberlin German. The audience went wild.

To return to Fussell's article: this visiting critic felt that the canonization of Wilder which he observed was a phenomenon that should interest the political psychologist. The Germans wanted a reassuring picture of America. *Our Town* supplied an image that was "pastoral, complacent, coy, charming, and entirely unreal." But according to this reporter, this was "an America which was becoming less believable every day." The Wilder vogue was significant of a new postwar condition of the German psyche which had passed from wallowing in the emotional fevers of the Nazi period into a phase of idealization and sentiment.

It is interesting that in this situation Fussell makes so much of *Our Town* and hardly mentions *The Skin of Our Teeth*. The impact of the latter on the German psyche, self-understanding, and will to survive was much greater, and this had nothing to do with bucolic escape, either American or German. How, moreover, does the thesis account for the extraordinary appeal of *Our Town* in Italy in these years?

This particular specimen of the history of criticism has been worth attention because it illustrates a wider phenomenon. Fussell's analysis is dictated by a doctrinaire premise whose modish character betrays itself in the self-assured rhetoric. *Our Town* is cartooned as "Old Folks at Home." This polemic vein of literary modernism, moreover, was often, as here, sidetracked by ideological considerations. As so often in Wilder's career, preoccupations with extraneous issues (socialism, plagiarism, etc.) obscured properly aesthetic assessment. In this instance, as in the case of Michael Gold's attack on the early novels, it was a question of my brother's social and cultural allegiances. Fussell could hardly have so misinterpreted *Our Town* were it not for an overriding ideological criterion. Its dramaturgy is certainly not realistic, and its audiences whether at home or abroad have not construed it as a documentary.

It may appear disproportionate and anachronistic to make so much of an early article by this able critic. The assessment of Wilder's work in it is, however, revealing of a widely influential critical mode, and one which still continues. The presuppositions which underlie this author's *The Great War and Modern Memory* (1975) reflect the same aesthetic and political commitments. I have my own personal reasons for underlining this continuity. The picture of that war in which I served as a combatant is one that I do not recognize. Again I conclude that the imbalance of the portrayal is due to an ex-parte prepossession. "Modernism" despite its services in deconstructing and unmasking the past has its own limiting dogmas. In Fussell's book the war and its aftermath in the public imagination are seen, indeed, in a justly disabused way yet in a way which is also simplistic. Frederick Pottle has characterized this mode as "Gothic."

I dwell on this telltale instance because I find it illuminating with respect to certain schools of criticism. Many of those reactions to World War I which Fussell documents so richly from his English poets should not be assigned the representative importance he reads into them. His weightings and emphases are governed by a special modish perspective. Just as emancipated circles in this country mistakenly allowed the World War I writings of Hemingway, Dos Passos, and E. E. Cummings to shape their view of the American role in that war, so Fussell operates more widely with his poets—though he hardly does justice to the greatest of them, David Jones.

No doubt important shifts of our modern outlook, syndromes of mental habit, go back to World War I and to those who first found language for that experience. But his selection is too partial. *The Great War and Modern Memory: whose* memory! As I have suggested, there are some of us still alive who took part in that war, also in the ranks, and we do not remember either the visage of war or its politics as Fussell's book presents these,[25] not to mention the noncombatant, ringside reportings of Hemingway, Dos Passos, and Cummings.[26]

No doubt the deglamorizing of war came to pervade modern society uniquely as a consequence of World War I. And no doubt a new realism and disenchantment diffused themselves through our general public with respect to the economic and political factors which lead to war. But the import and legacy of that ordeal cannot be captured in the partial evidence canvassed by Fussell. Too often, in any case, the reactions of the poet and artist in arms are determined by an apolitical and aesthetic stance, like that of some of our first American writers confronted with that war who sought a "separate peace." On the other hand, the same kind of talents caught in the ordeal may be specially exposed to ideological revulsion, anarchist or Marxist, as in the case of Dos Passos at the time.

I pursue this matter because here is one area in which avant-garde perspectives often reveal their superficiality whether as regards history or society. Moreover, in construing the lot of the soldiers, known or unknown, who fell in that war as marionette-victims of particular villains—generals, statesmen, social classes—they do less than respect to our fallen. I return to the witness of the greatest English poet of World War I, David Jones. For him, as indeed for the American combatants as I knew them, service in that war meant a willing participation in a conflagration or Armageddon or rite, inexorable but serving some proportional end. This disposition, which provided some sort of horizon for the tedium, duress, and fraternity of war, rested on ancient charters of a kind which no new iconoclasms could infringe.

All this is relevant to my discussion of my brother and his Americanism, not to mention his volunteering for service in World War II

---

[25]Cf. Frederick A. Pottle's review of the book in *The Yale Review* LXV, 4 (Summer 1976), 578–83.

[26]Here see my "At the Nethermost Piers of History: World War I, A View from the Ranks," in *Promise of Greatness: The War of 1914–1918*, George Panichas, ed. New York, 1968, pp. 344–357.

as a matter of conscience. His writing and outlook while disabused transcended ideological lines, and while committed to art were never apolitical or elitist.

I have mentioned the early wide appeal of *Our Town* not only in Germany but in Italy. As regards Italy and other European centers it is apropos to cite a letter from my sister Isabel, written in January 1946, a letter all the more interesting because it reflects immediately the responses to this play and the surprises of its reception in this period.

> In 1939 it [*Our Town*] was done in Rome by Elsa Merlini, leading Italian actress who has her own company. The opening night a leading Fascist politico tried to stop the performance, he and his group in the audience starting catcalls and speeches. Merlini came to the front of the stage and above the uproar asked the audience if they wanted her to go on. They cried, yes, yes, and the rebels were thrown out. Their complaint had been that it was an anti-Fascist play . . .

> Merlini has toured Italy for years with it in her repertory; ''Piccola Citta'' is a household word . . . Thornton was told by her and others that many Italians did not completely understand Acts I and II, but they adored and understood Act III and waited patiently for it. Shades of Dante!

> It was done long ago in Zurich and was a great success, ditto *Skin of Our Teeth*. Sweden. Buenos Aires. Pirated and performed in Spain. It was the first foreign play to be done in Berlin shortly after the Occupation. The Russian authorities stopped it in three days. Rumors gave reason it was ''unsuitable for the Germans so soon—too democratic.'' It is now in the American Section. We have heard direct—the program and reviews from Munich. Wonderfully played there. A great and moving success.

> A letter from our Swiss agent who handles the German translation says it is being done everywhere in Germany—they somehow get the script and do it. Yugoslavia asked Thornton for it when he was there—in the interests of cultural relations. Budapest. Czechoslovakia. The requests come in every day . . .

> Today I am answering a letter from the University of Delft. The University is having a festival to celebrate Holland's liberation. They

want to do *The Skin of Our Teeth*, saying it speaks for them, the whole world at this time rising out of ruins. Our authorities in Japan have written for permission to have *Our Town* translated and given to the native Japanese theaters for its importance *re* the American and democratic way of life and the art and literature it represents. Etc. Etc. It was done in the prisoner of war camps . . .

Such widespread success of the plays suggests that even in Germany one must look more deeply than Fussell did for an explanation. The evidence, moreover, is against his view that the enthusiasm was confined to the undiscriminating populace. This issue as to the particular factors in the acclaim is more interestingly stated by S. S. Prawer, the Germanist of Oxford, in his book, *Comparative Literary Study: An Introduction* (1973).

Wilder's plays also helped to bridge a gap in Germany's own severed tradition; for their techniques were inspired by those of the European avant-garde of the twenties and early thirties, the techniques of the Expressionists, in fact, whom Hitler had proscribed as degenerate and whose work was now becoming available again. Germans repaid Wilder with a critical acclaim which even in an intelligent work like Peter Szondi's *Theorie des modernen Dramas* (1956) must seem to English-speaking readers as excessive as English acclaim of Gautier's *Mademoiselle de Maupin* seemed to cultural Frenchmen at the end of the last century.[27]

In a footnote the writer adds the further observation:

Veneration of Wilder is not confined to critics or to Germans: the Swiss dramatist Friedrich Dürrenmatt ended a speech accepting a doctorate at Temple University with the words: "I close with the expression of my opinion that your Thornton Wilder is one of the greatest contemporary authors.[28]

What the actual vicissitudes of Wilder's critical reception were in Germany can be documented. I have in mind Heinz Kosok's "Thornton Wilder: Ein Literaturbericht," published in the *Jahrbuch*

[27] P. 28.
[28] Prawer here cites *The Journal of Modern Literature* I (1970), 91.

für Amerikastudien 9 (1964), and an article by Horst Frenz, "The Reception of Thornton Wilder's Plays in Germany," to be found in *Modern Drama* III (1960). These and other works on twentieth-century fiction and theater in Germany and many monographs on my brother's writings show that, already at the time at which Fussell wrote, his work received highly appreciative assessment both in academic and literary circles. I myself spent two semesters in 1951 and 1952 in the English Seminar at the University of Frankfurt and was guest lecturer in the corresponding Seminars directed to British and American studies at such universities as Cologne, Marburg, and Munich. In these faculties such established scholars as Papajewski (Cologne) and Walther Fischer (Marburg) and younger *Dozenten* like Franz Link, Helmut Viebroch, and Ursula Brumm were giving favorable and sophisticated attention to my brother's novels and plays.

It is true that properly aesthetic analysis of the writings in Germany was clouded and delayed by other factors. Quasi-political, ideological, controversial issues inevitably came to the fore in connection with the situation in Germany in these times. Attention was diverted to Wilder's personal impact and popularity, his ideas about democracy, the religious and philosophical aspects of his writing. The fact that his works were pushed by the American reeducation program and later by the German educational curricula had its ambiguous aspect.

Echoes of critical controversy in the United States were to be heard. Notable here were certain contrasts. Where Wilder's borrowings ("plagiarism!") of classical or modern material became a red herring in American discussion, in Germany this could be seen as a plus. As early as 1940 the German poet and critic Holthuzen had defended Wilder against charges of sentimentalism, and later (against Mary McCarthy) he defended *The Skin of Our Teeth* as a "convincing attempt to make great world theater out of contemporary stylistic resources." Szondi in his work on the modern drama mentioned above in terms I have cited had hailed in *Our Town* "the emergence of the poet" in the theater of our century by a return to the world theater of the Middle Ages and the baroque period. It was in these terms that he identified both the epic aspects of Wilder's drama and its character as living experience rather than allegory or homily.

VIII

Now that an English text of *The Alcestiad*[29] is available we can await with interest its eventual production in this country. It was well received by the audiences at the Edinburgh Festival in 1955 where it was entitled *A Life in the Sun,* though it was severely dealt with by London reviewers including Kenneth Tynan. In its German productions in 1957–1958 the play received wide attention and varying appraisals. Since then German studies of Wilder's work as a whole, books on modern drama, and inquiries into the use of classical material by modern writers, all have shown special interest in this latest version of the Alcestis saga. They have related the undertaking not only to the Euripides model but to modern reworkings reaching from Wieland's operetta (1773) to von Hofmannsthal, and in English from Robert Browning (''Belaustion's Adventure'') and Theodore Morrison to T. S. Eliot, who pointed to his use of this thematic in *The Cocktail Party.*

In *The Alcestiad* and his accompanying satyr play, ''The Drunken Sisters,'' Wilder draws on aspects of the saga absent in Euripides. His interest is in the duel between Apollo and Death. Not only is the heroine rescued by Hercules from the underworld, but thanks to her acquired wisdom and services to her city, after new vicissitudes, she is led at the end of her life by the god into the grove of Apollo. The portals of Death have been shaken and it is suggested that she is the forerunner of innumerable others to follow. As Apollo announces to Death, he has come to ''set a story in motion,'' that is, a new story in the relations of gods and men. Christian echoes are recognizable in the heroine's sacrifice for her husband, Admetus, and also in her life as ''servant of servants.'' Yet all is cast in the archaic Hellenic setting.

If this is again in some sort a morality play, yet it speaks at several

[29] New York, 1977.

levels and reconciles disparate elements. Our own contemporary actuality shows through the ancient fable, though not in the ironic modernizing way familiar to us in certain French dramatists. As in *The Ides of March* so here, Nietzschean and Sartrean nihilism is recurrent as for example in the way in which the ambiguities of the Delphic oracle are burlesqued. The ancient and modern servitude of woman is implicit in the aspirations of the heroine. Alcestis has shunned the yoke of marriage in the hope of serving Apollo as priestess at Delphi. She does not wish to live and to die "in ignorance." She learns that it is through the long detour of marriage to the king of Thessaly, with its "thousand cares" and renunciations, and through a reconciling and liberating role in the city, that the goal is reached and the new story set in motion. Käte Hamburger, in her book on classical figures in modern drama, *From Sophocles to Sartre,* observes that "Wilder's work is the most significant interpretation of the [Alcestis] theme in modern world literature."[30]

If this play were to be produced in this country perhaps the best initial sounding board for it would be found in schools, colleges, and private groups. I like to think of it as my brother's *Esther,* remembering that Racine wrote that play for the girls in a convent school. Referring to the first announcement of *A Life in the Sun,* he wrote me:

> That's *The Alcestiad,* but the entrepreneurs hate that for a title. That [*A Life in the Sun*] is a pretty cheery title for a play fraught with dire events, but it says that Alcestis's life is rooted in Apollo and there's a great deal about his being the Sun, so there you are . . .
>
> I hope that the High School graduating classes will be putting it on for years to come . . . The play is not all good but there are some beautiful passages. Besides, like its predecessors it *attempts* to succeed as such an out-size project that its coming short will be respectable but not disgraceful. As Hercules says in it—as he prepares to descend to the underworld to bring Alcestis back, ". . . and if I fail it will not be in a small thing." (The whole play is written in monosyllables almost.)

[30] New York, 1969. Translation of *Von Sophokles zu Sartre: Griechische Dramenfiguren antik und modern.* Stuttgart, 1962.

If *The Alcestiad* may, with whatever greatness and flaws, be destined for a particular kind of public, something of the same may be said of his work generally. The kind of bold improvisation, not to say effrontery, represented by his undertakings carries great risks both as to accomplishment and as to audience. For those to whom the concern, the locus of the action, is a matter of indifference, the work as a whole will seem to miscarry and any insufficiency will be damning. When, however, the theater of the play or novel corresponds to the inner theater of the beholder any flaws in the daring poiesis lose that importance.

The great question is whether some bolder reach is attempted. We may recall from *The Bridge of San Luis Rey* the comment of the narrator on the rehearsals of the Perichole and Uncle Pio:

Only perfection would do, only perfection. And that would never come . . .
Whom were these two seeking to please? Not the audience of Lima. They had long since been satisfied. We come from a world where we have known incredible standards of excellence, and we dimly remember beauties which we have not seized again; and we go back to that world. Uncle Pio and Camilla Perichole were tormenting themselves in an effort to establish in Peru the standards of the theaters in some heaven whither Calderon had preceded them. The public for which masterpieces are intended is not on this earth.

The outsize undertaking, the wrestling with a world of meaning and beauty which is only dimly remembered, with all the hazards involved, these are further suggested in two statements by my brother, the first with reference to *The Alcestiad:*

On one level my play recounts the life of a woman—of many women—from bewildered bride to sorely tested wife to overburdened old age. On another level it is a wildly romantic story of gods and men, of death and hell, of resurrection, of great loves and great trials, of usurpation and revenge. On another level, however, it is a comedy . . . about the extreme difficulty of any dialogue between heaven and earth, about the misunderstandings that result from the "incommensurability of things human and divine."[31]

---

[31] Cited in Rex Burbank, *Thornton Wilder*. New Haven, 1961, p.124.

Again, at the close of his Frankfurt address, "Culture in a Democracy," he spoke of the task of a democracy and therefore of its writers, "namely, to create new myths, new metaphors and new images, and to disclose that new order of values into which mankind has entered."

The observation of Proust which I have cited as epigraph speaks of the "analogy between the instinctive life of the wider public and the talent of a great writer," and implies that greater reliance can be placed on the response of such a public than on that of the "official judges." This might be construed to mean a pandering to Philistine taste, but Proust has in mind a deeper register of recognition.

In citing Proust's remark it is not my intention to disparage the modern critical movement as a whole. But our postmodern situation has brought two considerations home to us. For one thing—and we can use Octavio Paz's version of the matter—the modernist and avant-garde epoch has paradoxically undermined and annulled itself and its premise and brought it to a point of convergence with ancient and universal archetypes. In the second place, our own American reality can no longer be subsumed under large generalizations about the vicissitudes and fate of Western culture. In both respects the art of Thornton Wilder witnesses to a deeper ground which again would account for its continuing human appeal both at home and abroad.

Nor in citing Proust do I wish to make exaggerated claims for my brother's distinctive contribution. As with varying aspects of nature, so with works of rare artistic excellence: they are incommensurable. Criticism of real stature is less concerned with rank than with delight and understanding. Nevertheless, the point made by Proust has its validity in this instance.

The official judges with their changing criteria understandably have their excited attention drawn to voices of the time or moment, oracles of change, especially to new talents and special virtuosity. But there are two things that can be said about talent. For one thing society is prodigal in talent; one dazzling talent succeeds another. So it is that one reputation succeeds another every six months, one master eclipses another every decade, and one school replaces another every generation. The other thing to say is that sometimes talent or virtuosity is combined with something more, some further stature or scope or power of conception, and this is both rare and disturbing.

For those excited by talent or contemporaneity all such untimely or timeless works will appear austere or insipid. But in its marrow human nature senses unerringly what is important. All about us—yesterday, today, tomorrow—there is an unrecognized court in the hearts of men and women which sifts the arts of an age and gives its suffrage to whatever provides us with "incentives to go on living" (spoken of Ezra Pound) and whatever breaks through our modern fates.

SUPPLEMENT

The following address by Thornton Wilder, to which I have made a number of references, was given on October 6, 1957 in the Pauluskirche in Frankfurt on the occasion of the award to him of the annual Peace Prize of the Association of German Publishers and Booksellers. This award had been initiated in 1950. Previous recipients had included Roman Guardini, Martin Buber, Hermann Hesse, and two who were present on this occasion, Albert Schweitzer and Carl J. Burckhardt. Also present and greeted by the speaker were the President of the West German Republic, Dr. Heuss, the Mayor of Frankfurt, and Reinhard Jaspers, President of the Association.

The address was delivered in German but I use here Thornton's original English text as found among his papers with my acknowledgments to Donald Gallup, Curator of the Yale Collection of American Literature, and to Harper & Row who have included it in my brother's *American Characteristics and Other Essays* (New York, 1979).

CULTURE IN A DEMOCRACY

MANY ARE DEEPLY concerned about the preservation and survival of cultural values in the years that lie ahead of us: the Age of the Common Man, the Age of Democracy. They say: the gains which have been made—and which will be made—in the living conditions of the majority must be paid for by a loss in the conditions that encourage and produce superior works of the mind and spirit.

The danger is real.

In the previous thousands of years most artists, poets, and thinkers were dependent on the protection, encouragement, subvention of rulers, aristocracies, ecclesiastical hierarchies, and elites. What these privileged groups had in common, for the benefit of artists, were three things:

1. The relatively free disposal of their time. Most of them were not

all day in banks or offices or workshops, or in the fields. They had time to cultivate themselves, as we say. And from this experience of free time they had the insight: that artists and thinkers needed, above all things, uninterrupted time.

2. They ruled; they commanded; they were authoritarian. And from this characteristic in themselves, they had the insight to accord to artists a certain freedom in the choice of subjects and in the manner of their execution.

3. They felt themselves to be distinctly separated from the rest of mankind. Though relatively few in number, they felt under no obligation to consult the tastes or wishes of the majority.

In the society toward which we move there will be fewer and fewer persons enjoying these forms of privilege, wealth, authoritarian independence, and above all in possession of extended and uninterrupted time.

Already we see that the encouragement and subvention of cultural activities is in the hands of bureaucrats—of committees, of institutions, of foundations, and of governmental organizations—that is to say, of men and women who sit at desks from nine in the morning until late in the afternoon. The money they dispense comes very directly from the people and they must be very attentive to the tastes and wishes of the majority. The majority of the people are engaged in less cultural activities from morning until late afternoon.

This is the danger.

You have had experience in Germany of culture supervised by bureaucrats and Russia is having that experience now.

Another aspect of this problem is much discussed in the United States. We have more and more universities with twelve to fifteen thousand students. These institutions are supported by the taxes paid by their parents. These taxpayers feel they have the right to influence the content of higher education. The administrators must be attentive to these demands. Can they maintain standards of scholarship under such pressures?

The leadership of elites is giving place to the leadership of majority opinion. That is culture under a democracy. And our attitude to it depends upon our belief in the potentialities—the so-to-speak intuitive capabilities—of the average man existing in a democracy.

I am going to base my reply on some words of Walt Whitman—some very strange bold words.

He is discussing this problem in relation to the United States. But we may apply them to the situation everywhere in our Western world.

I have long felt that many of the manifestations we call Americanism would have taken place all over the world, even though the Western hemisphere had not existed or had not been discovered. Their source was in Europe—technological development, a classless society—the fugitives who came to the New World merely entered into conditions which produced an *acceleration* of such tendencies. The extent to which they received there a certain direction, a certain color, is the subject of another discussion.

Here are Walt Whitman's words:

> Of the great poems received from abroad and from the ages, and today enveloping and penetrating America, is there one that is consistent with these United States, or essentially applicable to them as they are and as they are to be? Is there one whose underlying basis is not a denial and insult to democracy?

He asks a question. What did he mean?

That the *Iliad* and the *Divina Commedia* and the plays of Shakespeare and *Paradise Lost* and *Faust*—were an insult to Democracy?

My friends, we approach a danger — cultural life under a democracy.

But we are also emerging from a danger. A danger that has hung over mankind for more than five thousand years: a poison, subtle and often sweet, that has been present in every activity of the cultural life and which is still present in the very structure of our language.

I shall try to show you that it has found its way into religious thinking, into our daily life, and into our assumption about the life of the family. That danger is withdrawing like bright-colored clouds from a sky at dawn; but it is present in all these "great poems of the past'' and it lingers under the surface of thought and feeling.

This was the insult: that God and destiny had given to a small number of persons an unearned superiority and that to the majority he had given an inferior lot; that *privilege* is not only in the order of society, but that it is in the order of nature; and in the order of divine governance. This was the feudal lie: that leadership is transmitted in the chromosomes; and that only communities enjoying these mystical privileges can produce and encourage and maintain all that is excellent, true, and beautiful.

But—you say—this is ridiculous. All that is long a thing of the past. Who takes seriously those kings and aristocracies and courts? We read about their marriages in the paper—and they resemble some childish marionette play.

Of the past?

But Mr. T. S. Eliot and many others still believe that only elites can produce an excellent thing.

And certainly we are profoundly indebted to those feudal elites for most of the treasury of culture. To Athens: one freeman to ten slaves. To the courts of Augustus, of Mantua, of the Medici, the Papacy, Charles, Philip II, Elizabeth I—to Versailles—to Weimar . . .

This fiction thrived by the help of a confusion of images—of metaphors. The Feudal Fiction reinforced itself by association with Divinity, Paternity, and the laws of gravity. God was a King and a Father; so all kings and fathers participated—by metaphor—in an element of divinity. God was above; and kings and fathers were above—and everybody else was *low.*

Since God was a Father, all men are children.

But God is not a King, He is spirit.

God is not a Father, He is spirit.

He does not wish us to be children, but to be men and women.

And as there are no more kings, it is now our duty not to be subjects, but to be co-rulers.

God is not above. He is within and over and under and around.

From this inextricable metaphorical confusion of God—King—Father—Above, we have developed the other confusion:

We are low, base, subject, childish, common, ordinary, and vulgar.

For a century and a half the majority of letters written in Germany were addressed as a conventional salutation to the ''Hoch Wohlgeborenen.'' (That is, to the ''Eminently Well-born.'') The rest of us were, by implication, the low-born.

One of the principal evils of this confusion was the image of the son. No man has a father after twenty-one. Lucky is the man who, after twenty-one, has in his father his best friend. A son until twenty-one is obedient; thereafter—not.

Notice the nations that have given to their country a feminine noun. They have even twisted a masculine word to make a feminine noun: *la patria; la patrie.* We speak of our mother country. A father one obeys; a mother one protects.

Notice how the feudal lie has embedded itself in the languages:

A view of a mountain is *herrlich* (i.e., lordly), *noble,* or *soberano;* and in English an evil act is *ignoble.* In English we speak of a ''noble experiment'' and a ''sovereign remedy.'' We hope our sons will be *gentlemen*—from the Latin *gens;* that they will show *gentility* and will be capable of *gentle* deeds. The word *common* (in German: *gemein*) ought to be a beautiful word. I would wish to associate myself with the *common,* the *ordinary,* and the *vulgar.*

Can't we save these words?

The evil that I am bringing to your attention is not so much that there were coteries of persons in high places, but that their jealous protection of their undeserved and unjustified privileges robbed the rest of the world of spiritual dignity—not only social dignity, but spiritual dignity.

We have all admired the phrase, *Noblesse oblige.* But have you observed the reverse of that famous saying—*Bassesse condamne?*

And let us remember for a moment all the other thousand-year-old lies that are gradually disappearing:

That a woman is incapable of responsibility in civil life;

That a woman in marriage has no rights in property and no rights in regard to her children;

That a man—under God and the state—may own and buy and

sell total ownership of another man;

That children, because of the accident of their birth in needy families, may be made to work from dawn to sunset;

That a man because of race or color or religion is an inferior creature—

Oh, the journey to truth and freedom and the maturity of man is not yet ended. The world is still full of sweet and comforting lies.

But the lie I have described is losing its strength.

Edmund Burke said that if you tell a man a thing a thousand times he will believe it.

Now, the mass of men have been told a thousand times a day that they were God's stepchildren; that He had His favorites and that those favorites were above them.

Democracy is not only an effort to establish a social equality among men; it is an effort to assure them that they are not sons, nor subjects, nor low—that they should be equal in God's grace.

It will take some time. Call men dogs for five thousand years and they will crawl.

Those bright-colored clouds are receding.

And how about culture?

Let us not be too easily frightened. We are confronted by some unknown factors: the characteristics of the Man with Head Raised. Extended over all society that is indeed something new.

Culture in a democracy has its dangers, but it has also this hope and this promise. It has a vast new subject to write about, to think about, to express, to explore: the Man with Raised Head.

That position, newly adopted, is uncomfortable and troubling— as some literature in recent years has shown us. It can even lead to despair.

Democracy has a large task: to find new imagery, new metaphors, and new myths to describe the new dignity into which man has entered.

SELECTED GERMAN BIBLIOGRAPHY

BECKMANN, HEINZ.   *Thornton Wilder.* Dramatiker-Serie. Velber bei Hanover, 1966.

————.   "Welt ohne Vater: Thornton Wilders Attacke gegen die Fundamente der abendländischen Existenz." *Rheinischer Merkur,* Nr. 2, January 10, 1958, p. 7.

FRENZ, HORST.   "The Reception of Thornton Wilder's Plays in Germany." *Modern Drama* III (1960): 123–37.

GERMER, RUDOLF.   "Thornton Wilder: *The Skin of Our Teeth.*" In *Das Amerikanische Drama,* ed. Paul Goetsch, pp. 170–82. Düsseldorf, 1974.

————.   "Thornton Wilders Bühnenstück *The Matchmaker* und seine literarischen Vorbilder." *Jahrbuch für Amerikastudien* XII (1967): 138–46. Also in Itschert, below.

HÄBERLE, ERWIN.   *Das Szenische Werk Thornton Wilders.* Heidelberg, 1967.

HAMBURGER, KÄTE.   *From Sophocles to Sartre: Figures from Greek Tragedy, Classical and Modern.* New York: Ungar, 1969. Translation of German original, Stuttgart, 1962. See ch. 6, "Alcestis," for Wilder.

HERMS, DIETER.   "Zum Humor im epischen Theater Thornton Wilders." *Die Neueren Sprachen* XX, 1 (January 1971): 36–47.

ITSCHERT, HANS, ed.   *Das Amerikanische Drama von den Anfängen bis zur Gegenwart.* Darmstadt, 1972. See chapters here on Wilder by Link, Stürzl, Haas, Germer, Lang, pp. 177–248.

KOSOK, HEINZ.   "Thornton Wilder: A Bibliography of Criticism." *Twentieth Century Literature* (July 1963): 93–160.

———.   "Thornton Wilder: Ein Literaturbericht." *Jahrbuch für Amerikastudien* IX (1964): 196–227.

KUHN, ORTWIN.   *Mythos, Neuplatonismus, Mystik: Studien zur Gestaltung des Alkestisstoffes bei Hugo von Hofmannsthal, T.S. Eliot und Thornton Wilder.* Munich, 1972.

LANG, HANS-JOACHIM.   "Ein Spiel von Göttern und Menschen: Vorläufige Bemerkungen zu Thornton Wilders *Alkestiade.*" In *Lebende Antike,*   ed. Horst Meller and H. J. Zimmermann, pp. 502–13. Berlin, 1967.

LINK, FRANZ H.   "Das Theater Thornton Wilders." *Die Neueren Sprachen* Heft 7 (July 1965): 305–18. Also in Itschert, above.

———.   *Stilanalysen amerikanischer Erzählkunst: Eine Einführung mit Übungen.* Frankfurt-am-Main, 1970. Section on Wilder.

———.   "Thornton Wilder: Ein Klassiker in der Moderne." *Der Rotarier* (Hamburg) 26, Heft 307 (June 1976): 383–87. Address, Freiburg im Breisgau, January 30, 1976.

———.   "Zeit und Geschichte in Thornton Wilders 'Wir sind noch einmal davongekommen' und Max Frischs 'Chinesischer Mauer'." In *Geschichte—Wirtschaft—Gesellschaft,* ed. E. Hassinger et al., pp. 31–39. Berlin, 1974.

LOTHAR, ERNST.   *Macht und Ohnmacht des Theaters.* Vienna, Hamburg, 1968. On *Our Town,* see pp. 146–49.

OPPEL, HORST.   "Thornton Wilder in Deutschland. Wirkung und Wertung im deutschen Sprachraum." Akademie der Wissenschaft und der Literatur: Abhandlungen der Klasse d. Literatur, Jahrgang 1976/77, Nr. 3. Mainz/Wiesbaden, 1977.

PAPAJEWSKI, HELMUT. "Die Problemschichtung in Wilders *The Bridge of San Luis Rey.*" *Germanisch-romanische Monatsschrift* VII, 4 (October 1957): 370–83.

————. *Thornton Wilder.* 2 Auflage. Bonn, 1965.

RIEGL, KURT. "Max Reinhardt als Vorbild für Thornton Wilders Caesar." *Die Neueren Sprachen* XVII, 7 (July 1968): 356–58.

ROSS, WERNER. "Klassik als Gegenwart." *Frankfurter Algemeine Zeitung,* December 9, 1976.

SCHÖPP, JOSEPH C. "Thornton Wilders *Our Town:* Theoretischer Anspruch und Künstleriche . . ." In *Amerikanisches Drama und Theater im 20 Jh.,* ed. A. Weber and D. Haack. Göttingen, 1971. Compares Wilder with Brecht.

STAIGER, EMIL. "Thornton Wilder." *Das Parlament* (Bonn) Nr. 31/July 31, 1976, p. 10. Also in the proceedings of the Order, Pour le Mérite, *Reden und Gedenkworte.* Heidelberg, 1976/77. Eulogy at Annual Meeting of the Order, Pour le Mérite, Bonn, June 2, 1976.

STRESAU, HERMANN. *Thornton Wilder.* Berlin, 1963. See also English translation, New York: Ungar, 1971.

STÜRZL, ERWIN. "Weltbild und Lebensphilosophie Thornton Wilders." *Die Neueren Sprachen* IV (1955): 341–51. See also Itschert above.

SZONDI, PETER. *Theorie des modernen Drama.* Frankfurt, 1956.

TRITSCH, WALTER. "Thornton Wilder in Berlin." *Living Age,* CCCXLI (September 1931): 44ff.

VIEBROCK, HELMUT. "Thornton Wilders *The Eighth Day:* Hauptmotiven und Schlüsselbegriffe," in *Der amerikanische*

Roman im 19 und 20 Jahrhundert, ed. Edgar Lohner. Berlin, 1974.

VON FRITZ, KURT.   "Euripides *Alkestis* und ihre modernen Nachahmer und Kritiker." In *Antike und Abendland,* ed. Bruno Snell and U. Fleischer. Band V. Hamburg, 1956. This book was written too early to include discussion of Wilder's version of Alcestis, but is valuable for its exploration of the problems involved. See Kuhn's book, 1972, listed above.

WILDER, THORNTON.   *An die Jugend.* Zurich, 1955. Includes "Goethe und die Weltliteratur."

————.   *Die Alkestiade.* Frankfurt, 1960. German translation of the unpublished Edinburgh Festival play, *A Life in the Sun.*

————.   Introduction to the English edition of Richard Beer-Hofmann's *Jacob's Dream.* New York: Johannespresse, 1946.

————.   "Kultur in einer Demokratie." Frankfurt-am-Main, 1957. Peace Prize address in the Pauluskirche, Frankfurt, October 6, 1957, at the award by the German publishers. For discussion of this controversial address, together with the text of T. S. Eliot's letter replying to the identification of himself in the address with an elitist position, see *Die Zeit* (Hamburg), November 14, 1957 (Feuilleton, Nr. 46, S. 11). See also the critical article by Rudolf W. Leonhardt in the same journal, October 17, 1957.